A Farmer's Lot

Roger Evans

MERLIN UNWIN BOOKS

Published by:
Merlin Unwin Books Ltd
Palmers House
7 Corve Street
Ludlow
Shropshire SY8 1DB
U.K.

www.merlinunwin.co.uk

The author asserts his moral right to be identified with this work.

Designed and set in Bembo 11pt by Merlin Unwin
Printed in Great Britain by MPG Books Ltd

ISBN 978 1 906122 47 8

To all of my family and my
friends in the owis Arms

Autumn

It's a nice sunny Sunday afternoon and I've been to feed the calves and look at the dry cows. Driving slowly home, there's a man with a telescope just inside one of my fields. I've seen him about the area before, it's always seemed obvious that he's watching wildlife but this is the first time I've had chance to speak to him. So I ask him what he's doing, not as in 'What do you think you are doing in my field?' but as in 'What has caught your attention, because I'm interested?' So he tells me that he's heard that there are some hobbies in the area. Hobbies, he tells me, are small birds of prey of a similar size to kestrels or sparrowhawks. So that's news to me and he goes on to tell me that he monitors the red kites in the area and that his telescope is so powerful that, should one alight in one of the trees around this field (and it's a 25-acre field), he could read its tag.

So we talk about red kites and I tell him how they have gone from one occasional pair to several in just a few years. He obviously knows that anyway, if he's monitoring them, so I ask him at what stage he would consider that there were too many kites. He says that would be when there were no crows or magpies left because that's what kites largely feed on. I tell him that that would be a good thing and he says that he thought I would say that.

So already in a congenial conversation, we are setting out our markers. Privately I think that if I were reincarnated as a red kite I would find easier prey than crows and magpies. So I tell him about how the skylarks have declined on my top ground. Without preamble he says, 'So you've changed your farming system then.' I find this so annoying: it is a given assumption that farmers are to blame. So I am able to tell him that the system is just as it has always been.

So he asks me why I think the skylarks have declined and I tell him 'red kites, buzzards and badgers.' He ignores the first two completely, no surprises there. 'I think you are wrong: a badger always travels across a field in a straight line so the chances of it coming across a skylark's nest on that line are very remote.'

I tell him that when I fetch the cows in, in early mornings in the summer, I can see how badgers have been busy because I can track their movements in the dew as they work a field comprehensively, and that I know it's badgers because I can see where they've turned dung pats over looking for grubs. He tells me that he thinks I must be mistaken. So no common ground there then. We say goodbye and I reflect that the encounter has been very much like the encounter I have with opposition supporters at the rugby club. We are all decent, likeable people, we'll have a drink together after the game, but while the game is going on, we see things completely differently.

★★★

A few years ago I was out visiting farmers in West Wales. I was being taken around by a farmer in that area. It was in January and it was a foul day. The cloud cover was low, it had rained steadily all morning, and some of the raindrops were white and drifted down in a more leisurely fashion. You knew, because it was such a raw cold day, that by the evening, and with just a slight drop in temperature, it would all be coming down white. It wasn't a good day for what we were about either. Farmers were outside in this weather, clad in most of the clothes they possessed and were not that inclined to take off all their outdoor gear and take you into a warm kitchen.

We, for our part, did not have the luxury of several layers of clothes and what conversations we had were of a shivery sort and the return to the car and its heater was welcome. So I didn't need much encouragement when my companion pulled up outside a pub and suggested we have a bar meal. The man I was with was a bit of a local character and he was made very welcome by the ten or so folk in the pub, most of whom also seemed to be farmers. I was introduced all around, ordered fish and chips and backed myself into a corner to watch life and people. It was grand in there, a roaring fire and the rest of the company were all in animated conversation and I enjoyed just watching. To my right hand was a large window and a tractor pulled up outside. It had one of those big spikes fitted to the back, that farmers use to take big bales of silage around when they are feeding cattle in the winter. The farmer gets off and he is clad in his waterproof trousers, wellies and waterproof coat as well though, as I was soon to find, he isn't wet because his gear has done its job.

He comes into the pub, and is greeted by all the company, he takes off all his gear including his wellies and as he makes his way across the bar in his stockinged feet to the toilets, presumably to wash his hands etc, he makes a small diversion to be introduced to me. I'm watching the landlady while he's gone and she pulls a pint of Guinness, unbidden, then while it is settling she goes to the whisky optic and takes two pulls at that, puts it next to the Guinness, which she tops up.

My tractor driver returns, knocks back the whisky in one go and then sips away at his Guinness. I'm in that pub for an hour watching what goes on. During the hour he has five pints and ten whiskies. So when we get back in the car, I ask my companion about him. 'That's his farm there.' It's a job to tell if the pub is in the farmyard or the farm is in the pub car park, they are so close. I ask about the Guinness and the Scotch. 'That's what he always drinks; he's in there every lunchtime and every night. He pays by cheque once a month and the bill is always over £1,000.' (5 years ago!) 'How can he afford that?' I ask. 'It's not bad, he makes the cheque out to the landlord by name and has him on his books as a self-employed shepherd.'

SEPTEMBER 18ᵀᴴ 2010

My wife had a big birthday the other day. She said that there were three things that she didn't want. She said she didn't want another corgi (We've been 'corgi-less' for six months now since Toby committed suicide under the electrician's van). She said she didn't want a party. She said she didn't want the bloody birthday anyway. There was nothing at all she could do about the latter; but the first two fell within my remit.

Never very good at doing what I'm told not to do, I made enquiries for a corgi at an early stage. Not that easy to find, corgi pups, but I did eventually locate a litter on a dairy farm in West Wales. They weren't ready to leave their mum at that stage so we had a three-week-long negotiation, I've still not come to terms with the cost, (because buy it I did), how much a kilo it must have been was beyond belief! I struggled to knock them down on price until I happened on another advert for the same pups in a different newspaper at a lower price, which was the price we settled on.

So now we've got this lovely little corgi bitch puppy, intent on wrecking the kitchen, and it seems strange to have to go through all the old routine of being careful where you step and putting your best shirts, that are due to be washed, well out of reach. Mert hates it and has given it the odd nip, just to establish a pecking-order; the puppy for its part is fascinated with Mert and follows him about endlessly. It must be the canine equivalent of being plagued by a wasp. Looking further ahead, Mert may have to go to the vets one day because sheep dog cross corgi pups are something I don't want but, as the pup is only as big as a bag of sugar, it's not something we need to worry about just yet.

The only part of the pup we haven't come to terms with is that it has a tail. It doesn't look right, probably because we are not used to it. I see old pictures of horses with docked tails and I think it's awful and docking dogs' tails surely comes in the same category so we'll have to get used to it.

The party took more planning, because we weren't to have one, it had to be a surprise. So I invited about 80 people to come at 2.30pm on the Bank Holiday Monday afternoon and at 2.15pm she knew nothing at all about it. She only knew then because some people came early. So all the food prepared by daughter and daughter-in-law appeared out of car boots, a barrel of beer came out of the back of my son's 4x4 and we were away. Surprises can be good.

★★★

I know this man who is a Holstein cattle breeder of some repute. He was asked last year, if he would go to judge the dairy cattle at an agricultural show in southern Ireland. If cattle breeding is your particular goal in life, invitations like this sort are the icing on the cake, because just to be asked is an accolade and a really nice sort of recognition and add to that a free trip to Ireland for a couple of days in such lovely countryside and a welcome from such friendly, hospitable people. So go he did, without needing much time to consider. He was met by his hosts when he arrived the day before the show and they had a good evening in the pub they had booked him into. Life did not come much better.

Next day, best suit on, he was collected and taken to the show and he set about his work. There are always lots of classes of dairy cattle, different ages, different breeds and he worked his way diligently through them all and then had to pick out various animals from different breeds as he compared one breed with another until he completed his work by selecting the best dairy animal in the show. It's a very demanding job and inevitably you don't please everybody, you just have to give it your best and job done.

He had chance to pause for breath, as it were, and reflect on the outcome of his efforts, with which he was pleased, and more importantly, he was confident that he'd got it right. Leaning on the rail as the last animals were led away, his host steward came up and congratulated him and thanked him for his efforts. 'I wonder,' said the steward, 'if you could help us out. You see, we've got a bit of a problem.' How can you resist such people; he'd enjoyed himself so much. 'Of course I will, I'll do anything I can.' 'Well,' and the steward leans closer as if about to impart a confidence, (which as we are soon to find out, he is), 'The problem is, the donkey judge hasn't turned up, and we wondered if you would judge them as well.' My friend is on full alert now, he can feel himself drifting into dangerous territory, 'But I've never owned a donkey in my life, I know nothing about them.'

The man leans even closer, looks furtively to right and left to make sure the conversation is still private, 'Yes, but there's only me and you that know that.' So my friend is eventually persuaded, charmed might be a better word, and to the best of his ability and not without some trepidation, he judges the donkeys. There's only one big class and he eventually lines them up in what he considers to be the right order. 'Well,' says the steward, 'That's grand, that's grand and no mistake, I can see you've got a natural eye for a good donkey. But if it's all the same to you, I'll put the rosette on the donkey at the other end of the line not this one, because the donkey at the other end, that you've put last, hasn't been beaten in a show for three years.'

★★★

As you know, I write these notes in the early morning in the kitchen, I've just been reminded that if there is a new puppy in a kitchen, it's a big mistake to walk about in your bare feet.

SEPTEMBER 25TH 2010

When we have calves born here they are allowed to suckle their mums for about three days. After that mums have to get back to work, produce milk to sell, and the calves can go either of two ways. Some of them go on to suckle 'aunties' which are usually older cows that are kept separately from the rest of the herd, just for this purpose. There are usually four or five aunties in this group with eight to ten calves and they live as a sort of commune and the calves take milk from wherever they will. Other calves move to a teat feeder where they are also in groups but in this case, milk is fed to them twice a day and they have to be taught to suck the teat. We have two groups of calves on teats: one group will become herd replacements and the other group are beef calves that we will sell at a month old. It usually takes 24 hours or two feeds to get the calves to switch from suckling a cow to suck this teat, they are fed twice during that 24 hours but usually need some guidance and help to make sure they are getting a proper feed. It's no big deal but it hasn't gone unnoticed that a popular time to move calves from cow to teat is on Friday afternoons, because it's me that has to do the training on Saturday mornings. Sometimes it's just the one calf, sometimes it's two, today it's eight!

This is quite a big job because you have to catch each calf and push it up to the teat, put the teat in its mouth and teach it to suck. When it's sucking you catch the next calf and so on. But it's not that easy because calf number one will stop sucking and fail to relocate the teat so you have to repeat the procedure endlessly. But I can cope with all that except that today there is a further complication. In amongst these calves, yapping and nipping away at them is our corgi pup. It's followed me up the yard for the first time, has shot under the gate into the calf pen without any hesitation and is creating chaos. I like a pup that will follow you about the yard without whinging at every puddle and whimpering at any mud, so I put up with the disturbance it is causing. We go back down the yard, Mert and I, with the pup hanging on Mert's tail. Could be that I've paid £400 for a fox?

★★★

I've made lots of mistakes in my life, and hope to make some more, but one of my recent ones was the buying of a 'new' Discovery. The man at the garage put me on to it, told me it was for sale and that it was in good order. And it is in good order, except for what is under the bonnet. It goes well for half an hour and then it boils. I've spent a lot of money on all the obvious possibilities and we are now left with the one that costs the most money, a cracked block. But not to worry, it will usually take me around the cattle OK but I've got two friends staying and they want to see hares. 'Where's all these hares you write about?' It's a hot day and we've not seen one: 'They are probably in the woods in the shade.' 'There you are, told you, he makes it all up.'

So we drive around several fields that are shut up for third cut silage and I show them lots of hares and that shuts them up. But it's a longer journey than usual and just when we are right on the top of the top field, the Disco boils over. 'What do we do now?' 'We walk down to the road and I'll phone for someone to fetch us.' And they get out and they go quiet. No complaints about the walk. They just stand and take in the breath-taking views; they can't get over how nice it is up here. I see it most days. I know how lucky I am.

SEPTEMBER 30TH 2010

I recently described the behaviour of our new corgi pup, towards Mert, my sheepdog, as similar in nuisance-value to that of an angry wasp. Enough is enough. Mert has lived quite contentedly in what we call our boiler house, a room just outside our kitchen door. The corgi for her part is very much an outdoor dog and moved in there with him. But you don't need a canine wasp pestering you all day and all night as well. So the corgi lives in the boiler house now in splendid isolation and Mert lives up the yard somewhere. Where he sleeps I'm not sure, he has plenty of warm dry places to choose from, but he's not happy about it. Luckily, justice in life is never very far away. Moles are back in to our lawn and I recently purchased a device that is supposed to move them on. It gives out intermittent vibrations and is put in a hole in the ground. So while I am making a hole in the lawn to put it in, I notice, just a yard away, another hole in the lawn which is the entrance to a very busy wasps' nest. I continue quietly with my work but the corgi pup, who is busily trying to eat the batteries I have with me, notices the wasps as well. In no time at all her nose is down the hole and she has been stung on the ear. Her cries of anguish bring the women out of the house. Mert, who is lying 20 yards away, gives just a flicker of a smile.

OCTOBER 9TH 2010

It's a raw cold wet day. The rain is driving at me on a blustery wind. It's as unpleasant as it ever gets in December or January and I need to remind myself, fairly regularly, that it is still October. I'm not best pleased. I'm not best pleased on three counts. It's the time of year when, gradually, your working apparel starts to change with the season. It's probably 12-13 degrees colder today than it was a couple of days ago. I've got a waterproof coat on, but there's little substance to it and underneath I'm shivering in a thin t-shirt. Today was the day I needed a 'working' pullover. I couldn't find one anywhere, I ransacked the airing cupboard before I came out, to no avail. There will be a row about that before the day's out, I will be on the receiving end of the row, the fact that I think that working pullovers should be close at hand will do little to help.

In the fields around me are fifty acres of cut grass, what we call third-cut silage. It's out there in the wet, just like me, and just like me it doesn't like it and it's spoiling. We had worked it out right. The weather forecast was right and the grass was right, so the grass was all cut, nearly 100 acres and the contractors gang would have picked it all up safely and easily in one day, before a belt of rain arrived. The same belt of rain that is falling on us, the grass and me, right now. But good plans often suffer little setbacks.

Next machine into the field after the mower is the rake. This gathers about 30 feet of cut grass in to one big swathe ready for the self-propelled chopper to gobble it all up. Rakes do a very fine job of gathering the cut grass together. I don't know if it's a design fault or not, but they are not so good at gathering electric poles. So yesterday the rake was wrapped around an electric pole, on another farm, and it took four hours to straighten it and mend it and that is the four hours that the silage gang lost that would have gathered my grass safely in. It's the sort of thing that happens in farming: you do your best, you make your plans and something totally out of your control contrives to spoil it all, and your crops of grass as well. I don't know who was driving the rake into the electric pole, but with very little effort, I could hate him.

★★★

However, believe it nor not, there are bigger issues at hand. The reason I'm out, wet and cold, is that we are TB testing. The cows are injected on Monday and the heifers, which are all over the place at this time of year, are injected on Tuesday. The cows were checked yesterday, Thursday, and today we are doing the dry cows and heifers. The milking cows passed the test, which came as a surprise. This, I had decided, was the year we would fail. The vet had told me that it was a case of when, not if. There's TB on farms all around me and, a bit like my grass, I had started to make plans in my mind that would cope with the difficulties of TB restrictions. The vet measures skin-reaction with callipers and every time she takes a bit longer with an animal, my heart starts its descent into my stomach.

But these cows are all clear and we move a couple of miles to the last 30 that are with the Limousin bull. And so we go on and on and we are down to the last heifer. I can't believe it; this heifer has to have several checks with the callipers. The last one! How ironic is that? But she's clear. I still can't believe it! Cold and wet, spoilt grass are forgotten. I've made crap silage before and will do so again. A warm pullover is found in the airing cupboard in about three seconds. All is well with the world.

★★★

Most of the cows around here are suckler cows. Beef-type that rear one calf a year and the calf stays with mother until it is weaned and mother prepares for her next calf. These cows live a free sort of life compared with dairy cows. They are obviously handled a lot less and inevitably some of them can be a bit of a handful. Limousin cross cows are reputed to be the worst but all sorts of cows can be a bit of a handful. I know a man who had Welsh Black cows with Limousin cross calves on them that were so wild they could never get them out of a field, so that if ever they wanted to move them they just left the gate open and hoped they would come out on their own. British Blue cows are reckoned to be quite docile and are now fairly popular around here. There are lots of stories about escapades farmers have with these cows but the reality is that if you have a wildish cow that needs some assistance to calve, well it's not funny, especially if you are on your own.

So it's caused a lot of amusement locally that one of my neighbours had ten or so cattle that he wants to sell (since the spring) and he can't get them home into his yard. They've been giving him the run-around for four months now. He did get them into a shed one day by mixing them with some quieter cattle but as soon as he shut the shed door, one of them jumped through the asbestos sheets at the other end and the others just followed through the hole it had made. So I think it's funny until I go around the heifers one afternoon and this group of cattle are in with mine. That's no big deal as far as I'm concerned, his cattle in my field this year, could be the other way round next. But as I've said, these are no ordinary cattle: when they see you they get up and threaten you. I phoned the keeper to warn him they are about. He has to go feeding in the dark mornings and I wouldn't like him to get caught out.

David and I go up to them one afternoon and from the safety of a four wheel drive we part our cattle from the visitors and drive them to a distant field. I phone the owner and tell him they are on their own now and he can fetch them. A few days later they are back on their own field. Story was, in the pub Saturday night, that the owner moved them on his quad bike. Story was, that one of the cattle jumped over both him and the quad bike and bent the handlebars. Story was, that the animal concerned was 600 kilos and it was chasing him at the time.

OCTOBER 16TH 2010

I was ecstatic that I had passed the TB test, (well the cattle passed it), but I still had those 50 acres of cut grass out in the wet. The next day was unbelievably dry, sunny and windy. The ground and all the grass dried out so quickly that the contractors were able to pick it all up in good order on the Sunday, and little harm was done. I only tell you this in case you were all really worried about that grass and were losing sleep. In the context of the weather we have had since, those were two almost freak dry days. Just have to be grateful for what we get and if it's good luck, make the most of it.

★★★

My daughter has a book of photographs of farming scenes taken in the first 20 years or so of the last century. I love looking at these old photographs but there are two in particular that draw my attention. The first shows a line of 14 Shire horses on their way to work in the fields. They are magnificent horses, harnessed together in pairs, and sitting sort of sidesaddle with each pair are seven waggoners who will work the horses all day.

The other photograph is taken on a downland farm with large fields in the background. It is 'bait' time, so several teams are drawn up at the top of the field, some have ploughs behind them, others have rollers and cultivators as they work the fresh ploughing down. Every horse has a nosebag on and a blanket over its back. The waggoners are resting as well, backed up to the hedgerow, to shelter from the wind, almost certainly eating bread and cheese and drinking cold tea from bottles.

I suppose we all have things that we regret in life but one of mine is that I never spent more time talking to men who worked the land with horses. There are plenty of people about with horses that can plough an acre at a ploughing match or demonstration at a farm museum, but men who went to work every day to work Shire horses, as they ploughed, sowed and harvested, are mostly gone. And inevitably their stories have gone with them. If you know of one, get yourself down there, or better still point him out to me. It's almost impossible for us to conceive what a hard life it must have been, but we can give it a good guess. So many of the things we take for granted would be missing.

Those men under the hedge taking their break would certainly be wearing hob nailed boots. If it was very cold, and it probably was, because most of this tillage work would be in the cold winds of March, extra warmth would come from the sack fixed over their shoulders and secured with a horseshoe nail. Rain would only stop them if the *land* became too wet, never mind how wet they were. No likelihood of a thermos flask to hold a warm drink. They would walk miles and miles every day, and think of the care and attention they would have to give their horses, so that they could do the same. Working horses were the ultimate in reducing the carbon footprint, not that that was an issue in those days. The power was bred on the land and the land fed that power for the rest of its useful life.

My wife's father would send two Waggoners to catch rabbits until the springtime came around. The sale of the rabbits would pay the rent! He would tell me a bit about working with horses, and he would have told me a lot more but at the time I didn't realise just how precious that knowledge was. I often tell stories I heard from a man who worked for me, Bill, but Bill was a groom. His world was hunters and riding horses, horses that pulled traps. He had his annual excursion with the travelling Shire stallion but he could never have handled a plough, for instance. He was of very slight build. The story was that he would have made a good jockey. He was starved as a child to give him the right physique, but no one ever trained him.

My father-in-law's highest land was on top of a hill; it was 40 acres altogether, two long narrow fields that straddled the crest of the hill. Down the crest itself was a long line of beech trees. He did tell me that when they were young, he and his brother would plough those forty acres with a single furrow plough each. I can see that line of trees from our yard. I've been up there in the spring when the east wind would cut you in half. I can only guess at the miles they must have walked to plough those 40 acres, with a plough that only took 12 inches at a time. I can certainly imagine them taking their lunch break, backed up against those same beech trees.

I wonder if they lit a fire from dead twigs to warm themselves. They would certainly have matches with them because they both smoked Senior Service at about 60 a day. I wonder about the detail. When they were ploughing, they would be walking in the flat furrow bottom, but later on they would have to work the ground down for roots or spring barley, so just how hard would it be to walk on that rough ground all day behind a cultivator? I wonder what my father-in-law thought in his later years when he would take a ride up there in his Land Rover to see how the ploughing was progressing with a 130hp tractor pulling a five furrow reversible plough at six or seven miles per hour. I wonder what went through his mind? One thing would be for sure, if he had his time over again, I bet he'd prefer to be on the tractor!

Presumably my own generation will also have stories to tell. Not for me, in my youth, the romantic picture of me perched on the back of one of a pair of magnificent polished Shire horses effortlessly moving off the yard to go to plough, sow, reap or mow. Off-hand I can't remember anyone coming to take a photograph of me with a wheelbarrow and shovel. When there was tillage work going on, I would be out there in the thick of it, but with a bucket picking up stones. My tillage work would be done in the evenings astride a little grey Fergie tractor. Not that it was important to work that land in the evenings: the importance came from the fact that I didn't get paid overtime. So if some earnest young person wants to know, I've got stories to tell.

OCTOBER 23ʳᴰ 2010

There's the *Big Issue* that you have the opportunity to buy in city centres, and there's the big issue of our kitchen table. At the one end of the table is a pile of newspapers, magazines and the post, which just grows and grows. As it grows it moves further down the table so the people sitting at the table have less and less room to eat. If it moves the other way it inevitably falls on the floor. It's a big issue because about every three weeks there's a bit of a row and a bit of a tidy up until the whole process starts over again. But, for this particular pile of various forms and paper, its time has come.

As I sit here writing (on the clear bit) I can hear our corgi pup working assiduously away, chewing one leg off the table. There are wood chips all around as it bites further and further into the wood. There's no point in stopping it, because it works away at it all night as well but when a piece of the leg falls off, as it surely will, it won't matter because, waiting at the end, and only needing moving to the corner, is the perfect counterbalance, our pile of paper. It will keep the table nicely balanced on three legs. I must check the corgi's pedigree; see how much beaver is in it.

★★★

I may have told you that our 'broiler' sheds now produce pullets that go, at point-of-lay, to outdoor laying units. Well, not long ago, one escaped. What shooters would call 'a runner.' So this lonely pullet makes its way into the farm buildings and lives there. It's been there five months now. It's obviously survived the attentions of any foxes about. Where it sleeps, we don't know. Its comb is bright red so it must be laying somewhere, but we are yet to find any eggs. You would assume that, as a lone bird living in isolation amongst the buildings, it would be living a solitary life, but creatures have a way of finding company, even with different species, and for the most part, our lonely hen is to be seen with or around the cows.

★★★

It's Sunday evening, we milk three times a day at the moment, and my son is on duty for the night milking. My conscience nags at me to go and help him, but it doesn't nag for long. What I do is go out on the lawn and put my dog Mert around the cows, to fetch them home, to save David some time. The corgi comes across the lawn with us. I am convinced that this corgi will become a cow dog. Once she sees Mert doing his work, she struggles through the fence after him and I think to myself, this is the start of her working career. But she discovers a kitten in some nettles and is distracted as she tries to do something unspeakable to it. Mert has the cows all heading in the right direction now and I stand and watch as they pass up the track about 20 yards from me. We've been cross-breeding for some time now as we try to breed a cow that will live a longer and contented life. So our cows are quite a mixture, a couple of black Holsteins, some all-black Swedish Red crosses, a roan Shorthorn, a fawn Jersey, and there, just visible in the deepening twilight, making her way in single file like all the others, is a brown hen.

★★★

We've been away one night to attend a wedding and it's early on Sunday evening. I could do with a quiet evening in the chair but our living room is dominated on television by people who can't dance. This makes me restless; it's a lovely evening so I start to think about what I could be doing outside. I remember that there are ten heifers in the wrong field that will need moving the next day. The first part of the move will take them from where they are into the succession of fields that comprise a small valley. What I want is for them to re-join their group right on the very top where they are supposed to graze off a field we need to plough for wheat. So I think to myself that, if I complete the first part of the move tonight, they will have probably made their way up to the top by tomorrow morning. We only have one old 4x4 that's roadworthy now and it's nowhere to be seen so I put Mert into the boot of my Honda and we set off. I've got to do a bit of planning now. I've got to get the heifers out of the field onto a farm road.

I've got to shut the gate behind them and then open an adjoining gate to send them down a track to the little valley. But if I've got multiple-choice options, so have the heifers. If they will come out of the field on their own, I reckon me and the dog will manage, but if they won't, well, I can only stop them going one way and my preferred option will be to stop them going down to the main road.

But I didn't get where I am today without a bit of ingenuity. One of the advantages of having a big old car, apart from the comfort and the performance it affords, is that, should the need arise, it can be placed in a strategic position that will block a lane off. So I shunt it back and fro until it fits neatly across the lane, the bonnet touching one hedge and the boot the other. Then I open the gate and call the heifers out onto the road. They come to the gate but will come no further. The next obvious option is to put the dog around them, which I do and the downside to this is that I've been away for the weekend and the dog has missed me. He, for his part, is determined to show me just how important he is in my life so that I don't go off and leave him again.

The heifers don't come out of the field at a trot; they come out of the field at a gallop. My car, the barrier, is 30 yards away, put there as a deterrent to going in that direction, not to be mistaken for the wall of a pen to be jostled against. But the heifers are in full flight, the first one there jumps up on the boot and off the other side and all the others follow it.

My first job now is to shut the field gate to reduce their future options by one. But Mert is still keen to make an impression and without any bidding he's gone under the car, off down the lane, overtaken the heifers, turned them back and as I get back into the lane they are coming nicely over the boot of the car again in the other direction. They set off quietly now down the track I want them to and the dog and I follow them. We shut the gate behind them; the dog knows he's done really well and keeps pushing his head against my legs for congratulations, which he gets. I put him back in the car boot, which will still open. It's getting quite dark now; I'll have a look at the damage in the morning.

OCTOBER 30TH 2010

So I'm driving up the track to our other land. I do it every day, but it's a slow drive today, because moving up the track in front of me is a carpet of partridge. I have a great affection for these little birds. It must be something to do with the busy way they scuttle about their business in their large coveys.

It's evening now and there are quite large numbers making their way to wherever it is that they intend to settle for the night. It's no wonder the keeper is so vigilant in his continual war against foxes, because these partridge would surely make an easy meal for the nocturnal fox, wherever it is they snuggle down in long grass or game cover. I've not seen the guns out after these partridge yet but it can only be a matter of time, and I expect to see them out on any Saturday soon.

NOVEMBER 6TH 2010

'Eighty four.' 'Eighty four what?' It's the keeper, he's been out lamping and he reckons that's how many hares he's seen. I've been a bit worried about meeting the keeper. The keeper's got a copy of my first book and he is probably mentioned more than anyone else, so I was just a bit wary. But it's not a problem. He likes the book and enjoys his role in it. So he is counting hares with even more enthusiasm. He tells me that there have been people caught coursing hares on the next-door estate and that he will keep a special eye out in future. I will as well. There's lots of signs you can read to see if there's been someone about. Is that puddle in a gateway clear and undisturbed or has someone driven through it, and if they have, who was it? The keeper uses what we call a mule

and it has a narrower track than a normal 4x4 so I always know if
it's him. Some gates I tie with string as well as use its catch, and
I tie the knot so that I can tell if someone else has undone it and
been through.

★★★

I took some calves to market yesterday. For the first time in over 12
months the lights were working on the trailer. For the first time in
12 months, I didn't have to plan my route so that it was nearly all
left turns. You can sneak off to the left with fewer problems than
turning right. I like to feel that during the year I played a part in
bringing back hand signals into this area. If I wind the windows
down in the Disco very far I can't get them back up again, and
who wants to drive about on a wet day with the windows down?

   When I got back home I felt really good about myself
because I'd been legal. I had a crap price for the calves but the
well-being outweighed that. On reflection, if a good day is driven
by having indicators on a trailer, is that a bit sad? I was thinking
recently about the huge value of the reminiscences of older people,
and in particular I lamented the fact that I had never spent more
time talking to horsemen. The coincidence was that a lady I'd met
at a milk meeting turned up next day to show me the books she'd
written about local history in the area where she lives, Stafford-
shire and the Peak District of Derbyshire. She should be so proud
of what she has done because she went to great trouble to record
older people's memories of their lives and the anecdotes that go
with those lives, in the person's own words. I'm reading one book
at the moment. It's enjoyable reading but more important than
that, it's an important work of local history which will be invalu-
able for generations to come. My own work often takes me into
that part of the country: the people are as nice as people you meet
anywhere. The scenery in the Peak District is spectacular; well
worth a visit.

I retired from my directorship of my milk cooperative a couple of weeks ago and this will mean a huge change in my life and indeed my lifestyle. My own motivation has always been to try to make things better for dairy farmers and it would be quite easy to say, with the current economics of dairying, I've not been successful. I've always thought that dairy farmers would be better off if they worked together. Working together is a way of acquiring power in the market place and when you think about it, not many people would want you to be successful. The processors who buy the milk wouldn't want it, the supermarkets wouldn't want it, and although they will never admit it, politicians wouldn't want it either. So it was always a big ask and slowly but surely I think that farmers working together in cooperatives will succeed. It will succeed because it works almost everywhere else in the world. And not all working together, as is the case in the UK at the moment, certainly isn't working either.

Over the past ten or twelve years I've had a diary that would make a lot of people cringe when they saw the miles and the hours involved in the directorship but now that much of that has gone, what for me? Well I've got my writing and I've got my farming and then I've got enjoying myself! For example I've not been out much at weekends because I needed to be on full power the following week. So I've started going to the pub in the village on Thursday nights, which is known as 'farmers' night' because they 'all' get in there. And I've started going to the pub on Saturday nights too because it gets me away from the television and people who can't dance or sing, and besides everyone else goes out on Saturday nights. So there I am at one o'clock on Sunday morning and there's two guitars going and we are singing *American Pie* and I've still got to drive home a mile and a half but not to worry because it's the time of night when people start drinking shorts whereas I'm on my third pot of tea with cucumber sandwiches.

Winter

I've never been much given to envy, but must confess to just a
touch of envy this week. We had a new member of staff a couple
of months ago. Seems a bit strange to describe him thus because
he's been a friend for years and years, lives in the village, and we
know him well. It's just that he's come to work for us instead of
someone else.

As a digression, a couple of weeks after he started here,
we hired a muck-spreader from a local contractor. The muck-
spreader carries the name of the owner in several places and our
man was seen locally with the muck-spreader behind a 'new'
second-hand tractor we've just bought. So the big story of the
week in the village is that 'I knew he wouldn't stick working
for those Evans long, he's already left and is working as a tractor
driver for Owens.'

Anyway, his main job here is to do tractor work and at odd
times when he's had an hour or so to spare, he's done an overhaul
of our plough. Not before time. Previously, ploughing has always
been a bit of a rush for us as we try to get ploughing done in just a
few hours between tending stock. But now it's different, Stephen
goes off to plough early in the morning and he knows he has the
whole day to devote to it.

This week he's been ploughing our top field. It's one
of our biggest fields, 25 acres, and his first furrows would have
been along the 1,000ft contour line. I went up to see how he was
getting on. There are 360° views, spectacular ones from up there.
The plough was fine, the ploughing was fine, the soil is remarkable up there and was turning over so well you could hardly see
the individual furrow lines. The tilth was so good you could have
drilled winter wheat straight into it. We need to lime it so we will

have to go over it once with the power harrow to take the lime spreader wheel marks out. Yes, I was a bit envious. It's not often in life you get to do such a fundamental job in such splendid isolation, with just hares and skylarks for company.

★★★

So I'm in the pub and we're discussing Christmas and New Year and the landlady thinks we should have a 'theme evening' one night. So the usual ideas are trotted out. 'Tramps and Tarts' is about the extent of most people's imagination. I suggest that this would be a non-event as most of the regulars would only have to turn up in the clothes they usually wear. So this triggers memories of a previous Tarts and Tramps night they had a few years ago. Apparently most people had made an effort and there were some very 'tarty' women there that showed a side that had been hitherto unsuspected. Never mind showing a lot more leg and bosom than was usual.

Anyway at about nine o'clock a local man pulls up outside on his way home from work. He parks his dirty van outside and takes himself and his dirty dog into the bar. He was the sort of man who washed and shaved about once a week, unless he was busy, when he skipped both chores and carried on 'til the next weekend. His clothes were normally so dirty that the landlady had said that if he ever leaned on the wall again he would be barred from the pub. (He always left an oily silhouette on any wall he leant on.) So he sits in the corner with his dog and his pint and his packet of crisps and to his surprise he is declared the winner of the tramps competition, without him really being aware that he was being judged.

Which recollection triggers off another! Our small local town has a carnival that, like most carnivals, ends in a procession and a day of activity on the sports field, but there is a week of events leading up to the big day and one of those, a popular spectacle, was a pram race. They don't have it now, I think because 'Ealth and Safety' took an interest. We all must tot up, some day, the full extent of their interference in our lives.

Anyway the idea was that two people pushed a pram from pub to pub and the occupant of the pram had to drink a pint of beer at each pub. It was all very light hearted on the surface, teams wore fancy dress and decorated the prams, but beneath all that it was hugely competitive. There would be two or three local soccer clubs who would all try to beat the local rugby club who in turn would be determined not to be beaten by the sort of pansies who played soccer, and there would be a couple of sinister teams, men well on into their thirties, serious drinkers who wore heavy boots and tattoos, best to stay well clear of them.

So my son and I and a local landlord decided we would enter this pram race but that it needed a new approach. It all started off outside one of the pubs with a sort of 'Le Mans' start and a frenetic rush to the first pub. Did I say we hired gorilla suits? Well, we did. So to the amazement of the crowd, while all the other competitors rushed off, we left our pram in the middle of the road and went into the pub and the three of us had a pint. We came out in leisurely fashion and set off in similar fashion for the first pub. We all went in for a pint and if it was a good pint we had another. All the other competitors would have finished by now; the winners would have visited eight pubs in about 12 minutes. The finishing line was in the village hall where a dance was being held. The M.C. of the dance interrupted the evening with news of our progress. 'The three gorillas have now left the *Boar's Head* and are going to the *King's Head* and are going back to the *Boar's Head*!' We eventually finished the course in 4½ hours. We didn't win a prize but we were the star turn! I fell down later that evening on licensed premises and broke my collarbone. I think the pub floor was uneven and anyway it was only the one collarbone. And I was younger then, mind.

★★★

We were talking about threshing the other day (alright, yes, it was in the pub). Some of us can remember the demise of the threshing drum as combines very quickly took over. It was common practise for a scrap dealer to buy the drum, to tow it out clear of the buildings, light a bale of straw underneath and come back a couple of days later to pick up all the metal that was left. Which was a shame, in a way, but it also spelled the end of a lot of backbreaking work that, with the passage of time, has become romanticised.

My own career with farmwork coincided, just, with the end of threshing. In south Wales where I was brought up, most farms were small family farms so neighbour had to help neighbour in order to create a team large enough to run 'the show'. As 'the boy' on the farm, it was mostly me that was sent to help out next-door or wherever. The first time I went I was put to throw the sheaves off the stack on to the drum. I soon learnt that there was just a bit more to it than that, that I had to toss the sheaves to the man cutting the strings so that they arrived in just a certain way so that he could feed them into the drum. After that particular severe bollocking I was soon comfortably into my work, working my way around the stack and throwing the sheaves down onto the drum. But the top of the stack where I was working soon came down to a level with the drum and just as inevitably, I had to throw them up. I was only 16.

My boss told me later that day that there should have been two men on the stack, that it was too much to expect someone of my age to handle all those sheaves on my own. Bloody right it was. Not that there would have been an easier option in the team. The grain came out at the other end into 2cwt sacks (that's 100kg) and had to be carried across the yard. The only concession to their weight was a sack lift that wound the sacks up to shoulder-height. The straw came out into a stationary baler where it was tied into huge bales with wire. There wasn't much respite either. There'd be a cup of tea, mid-morning and mid-afternoon and there would be the odd occasion where the drum would have to move to another bay, and of course lunchtime, but if you didn't bolt your food down, well, you didn't get chance to eat it. Otherwise it was a relentless pattern of work with the men feeding the drum, shouting to me for more sheaves, and nasty with it.

★★★

It was a 'given' in Wales at that time that if you worked on somebody's farm you were fed in the farmhouse. You weren't expected to carry sandwiches and flasks. I live on the borders and I've heard local farm mechanics say even today that if they go to work on farms to the west, they never need to get their food out of the van, go to the east and it's a different matter. Which tells you quite a lot, depending on where you live!

Anyway I went one day to thresh on quite a large farm and there was a mixture in the gang of farmers, smallholders and farm workers, but if you came upon them and mixed with them you would never be aware that there were any social differences. But the farmer on this farm was a retired army officer and we all had to call him Captain _____. When we went into the farmhouse for dinner (it certainly wasn't lunch) we found that we had been graded. Farmers ate in the kitchen proper, smallholders were in a sort of back kitchen and farm workers ate in the scullery. This caused great amusement because we could all see and hear each other and there were quite a few ribald comments flying back and fore. It was even better the next year because one of the smallholders had taken on two extra fields and this had moved him from back kitchen to main kitchen, to everyone's great amusement. You can guess the order in which the food was served! Where did I eat? I've always been in the scullery of life.

Another farm we went to when I was a lad was a big, rough farm. The farmer was big and rough and so were his two sons. His wife by contrast was a tiny little lady who had obviously come from a better background and who tried, to little avail, to bring some gentility to her life, in spite of the roughness of her surroundings and her male family. She loved having 'guests' to feed at threshing time and served superb food, put out serviettes and more than one knife. Everyone liked her and entered into the spirit of the thing. Everywhere else, all of the meal was put on your plate but she put the vegetables out in dishes and there were 'pleases and thank-yous' flying about in all directions.

We all tried to eat with some decorum while her husband and sons demolished their food in quick order, piling it into their mouths with fork and knife like JCBs, which had yet to be invented. She pretended to be oblivious to this but I'm sure she wasn't. She carried on presiding over this lunch, in her element. 'Roger, I'm sure you'd like another cup of tea, pass me your cup.' And she took my cup and saucer, filled it with tea. 'Sugar?' 'Yes, please.' Two spoons of sugar went in and 'you take milk, don't you?' And the spoon travelled down to her side and entered the half-hundredweight bag of calf milk powder that was standing on the floor beside her chair and she stirred the powder into the tea and passed me the cup back with a gracious smile.

November 27ᵀᴴ 2010

'What would be nice,' I said to myself at the end of September, 'would be a nice dry October, so that we could keep the stock out longer and shorten the winter.' Well we did get that good October and then a week into November as well. This week the weather has alternated between winter one day, with torrential rain and wind, and nice sunny days. But if you throw a few of those wet windy days in to three or four consecutive ones, well it's winter and no point in kidding yourself. So we've been bringing cattle in this week and the irony is that we've got grass everywhere. Lots of it. We've still got stock out, but it's a careful balance between them grazing the grass off and their feet damaging the sward.

So, Mert the dog and I have been busy with moving cattle about in the stock box and we've enjoyed it. We had to take two loads of young cattle to some other buildings we rent a couple of miles away, which is no big deal unless you meet another car on the way. The journey takes you down narrow lanes with few passing places and if you do meet a car, most drivers just sit there and expect you to back up with a trailer behind you. The only conclusion I can make is that they themselves simply cannot reverse although there are occasions when the nearest passing place is 40 or 50 yards behind you.

One day I had to take a load of straw and was expected to back up, so I did. I couldn't see if there was anything behind me. People around here are always complaining about the speed of broadband, or rather the lack of speed. They had plenty to complain about after the back of my load of straw took a telephone pole out, and they must have been even more frustrated that they couldn't complain properly because they didn't have any telephones either.

★★★

If you get well into the countryside around here there are isolated houses and cottages tucked away in nooks and crannies of dingles and into woods in places you would never suspect until you stumble upon them. Quite a lot fell into disrepair fifty years ago and were allowed to fall down, because at the time their value would never justify the renovation costs. There's many a heap of stones or bricks around which, had they been kept in some sort of order, would have been worth good money today. I suspect that they were built to house a shepherd or forestry workers so that they could live close to their work.

An isolated lonely life it must have been for them and

their families. There's a pile of stone just two fields away and I know people who lived there as children. On the skyline there is a vast wood and you can see, from here, a slight indentation in its silhouette, which tells you that it is in fact a twenty-acre field right in the middle of the wood.

Years ago I bought straw off that field and there in the corner, was a pile of stones that was once a cottage. Where they got water from goodness knows, let alone things like electricity that we all take for granted.

Just a few fields away from here is a rather grand house that was built out of red brick and consisted of just one room downstairs and one up. It housed a shepherd and his family and old Bill who worked here with me can remember, as a child, that the shepherd and his wife reared seven children there. They had to carry their water from a spring in a wood about a mile away and twice a day the wife would go to fetch water across the fields with her seven children trailing behind her in descending order. 'It looked like a sow and her piglets going across the field,' says Bill. Not very politically correct, a bit sexist, but then those things didn't exist either when Bill told me, and to be fair, his description does help to conjure a picture in our imagination.

★★★

My son thinks he's the boss on this farm. Everyone knows that I think I'm the boss, and we are both kidding ourselves. Our corgi pup has taken charge. She won't be a big corgi in size but she's big on character. Last Saturday I took her to fetch the cows home. There's a lane that runs through this farm which leads to our farthest field, so we go into the field and bring the cows home in front of us. The cows for their part haven't seen the corgi so close at hand before so they gather round for a closer inspection. The comparison in size is something like me compared with a double decker bus (just), but the corgi is undeterred. If the cow comes at

her head-on she gives ground, but just as soon as the cow turns
tail, the corgi is snapping at her heels.

　　The last part of our journey takes us up a track that has
become muddy as the season wears on; it's ankle-deep for cow or
man, for a young corgi pup it's half way up her body, but she continues
on undeterred. The cows are all heading in the right direction but
any that stop are given a good yapping and a nip on the heel. Which
is exactly what corgis were designed to do in the first place. So we
were having our tea last night and there's a bit of a smell in the
background. I get the blame initially because I've brought my dirty
wellies into the kitchen, which I shouldn't. I stomp off and put them
outside but the smell persists. So we go round the kitchen to try to
locate the smell. The corgi is fast asleep in her basket. There's not
much room for her because she's got a slipper in there, an old boot of
someone's, but cuddled up to her, or rather the other way round, she
is cuddled up to a dead rat. Not recently dead mind, several weeks
dead, almost mummified, but very pungent nonetheless.

★★★

All this bringing the cattle in for the winter has its downside. I
have to set my alarm for 3.30am Saturday and Sunday mornings.
This will be a norm for me now until the cows go back out. It
sounds appalling, and in a way it is, but the plus side is that I'm
lucky to be able to do it, so it's a positive in my life I think.

DECEMBER 4ᵀᴴ 2010

Nature is supposed to send you bull calves and heifer calves in
equal proportions. For some reason, we never get our share of
heifers: the last time I'd counted we'd had 50 bull calves and 15
heifers. If the calves are by a beef bull and destined to be sold on
at a month or so old, then it's no big deal and bull calves are worth
more than heifers. But to breed replacements that will replenish
the herd one day as cows, it's a big issue. Our aim, for all sorts

of good reasons, is to have a self-contained herd that replenishes itself: there are good bio-security and health reasons to justify this, and at the same time we seek to breed a more robust, less extreme dairy animal that lives a longer happier productive life rather than the short life, wasteful scenario that is seen in some cases. So if you don't get enough heifer calves, it's a very serious matter.

One bad year is bad enough but we are at the end of several bad years and our herd is getting older. 35 heifers would probably be OK but because we don't get and haven't had these numbers, we are at the stage when we could do with a couple of years with 40 or 50 coming in. I know lots of people who get lots of heifers, who have heifers to spare. I can only conclude that 'ours' are sent by second class and turn up somewhere else or get lost in the system. But it's no good just complaining, you have to get out and do something, so if we can't breed heifer calves, we must to buy some, the theory being that the sooner they join our herd, the better they will fit in with our vaccination regime and become accustomed to any bugs we have about.

Last month I bought ten, three month olds and last week I drove 60 miles to see six. These latter were crosses, a Dairy Shorthorn bull on a black and white Holstein cow, a very good cross and just the sort of animal we are trying to breed. So I see the heifers and we do a deal. The farmer says 'I've got three younger heifers, Shorthorn cross Jersey.'

I tell him I'm not interested but he wants me to have a look at them. You can't always tell how a cross breed will turn out and I've never seen this cross before and didn't know what to expect. They were beautiful calves, all like the proverbial peas in a pod, the colour of Guernseys. So inevitably I bought them as well: it's the big brown eyes that did it, but I've got to break the news to my son. So I describe these three calves to him, much as I've told you. 'Pity you didn't buy them as well.' Phew! That was a close one.

December 11ᵗʰ 2010

There's untold pleasure to be had from a dog. My relationship with Mert is well chronicled, but it seems there was still plenty of room in my heart for this little corgi bitch we've got. I can hear her growling outside the kitchen door now; I've just put the remains of some chilli con carne out in her dish and she's eaten the lot. She's growling at the cats as she sits by the empty dish, just in case I put some more out. I never thought a dog would eat it but she did and licked the dish clean. We once opened a tin of mandarin oranges that looked a bit 'iffy' and a previous corgi ate them all. She's so much fun to have about the yard, she's busy about the cows, the calves and in particular, the cats.

Yesterday there was a visiting tomcat about the yard. He looked a nasty piece of work, rough and tough and carrying the scars of previous battles. The corgi spotted him immediately and plagued him all morning as he moved from shed to shed seeking respite. She managed, the corgi, to miss the dangerous swipes of his claws, but that's been a learning process for her because her nose carries marks from where she has got too close to other cats. She eventually cornered the tomcat on the roof of a tractor and stayed proudly in the vicinity all day keeping an eye on him. At the end of the day she came into the house and the cat slunk off. I've deliberately not told you the corgi's name; it's a bit girly, not a proper name for a farm dog. I call her 'Foxy'.

★★★

'Is there anybody there?' It's a plaintive cry and it comes from one of the barn conversions on our yard. You can only hear the call for help; you can't see the source because the garden and the property are well screened by shrubs. But I know the voice well, it's the man who owns the house and I go to investigate. He owns two of the conversions on the yard and lets them out. One lot of tenants moved out yesterday and he's come to see what sort of state the house was left in. He's standing on the doorstep in his socks. He'd removed his shoes before he went in because they were a bit dirty and while he was making his inspection, his shoes have disappeared.

I've got a fair idea what has happened to them but still have to find them. I plunge in to the undergrowth of the shrubbery and there, under an evergreen tree of some sort, a kind of miniature leylandii , is a corgi pup with a shoe in her mouth. The other shoe is close by, it's a bit of a treasure trove I've stumbled on, also one of the slippers I lost a month ago and the hand brush we use in the dairy. The pup smiles at me, as they can.

DECEMBER 18TH 2010

I haven't been outside yet this morning but I was out yesterday, Sunday, long before the sparrows got up and I was out all day long. It was minus 14 here in the morning, which is too cold by some distance. It catches you out, that first real freeze. The parlour is long and open at one end and almost impossible to keep warm, so we don't try, we just go to some length to drain every little bit of it, but if it's as cold as -14, the tiniest drop of water resting in a tube is a barrier to milk flow. We just managed, then there's all the tractors on work-to-rule and it took some time to get them all going, but we manage as we always do.

The cows have four water tanks to drink from but we let them use only one and because there's a bit of a queue it's always running and it never freezes. We've got 21 dry cows out clearing some grass up, they've got some high-energy feed blocks as well but I decided they needed some dry feed too, so I took them a nice round bale of silage.

I had Mert the dog with me because I thought on a day like this they'll smell the silage and I'll have a job getting the feeder and bale into the field without them getting out onto the road. I put out both, I called them, just a couple lifted their heads up, the rest took no notice at all. You can take a horse to water etc! Last job of the day is to feed all the wild cats, a sort of feline winter fuel allowance.

There are three problems with getting old; one of them is the inability to remember if you've told someone something or not. I can't remember what the other two problems are.

I was using Mert to fetch my in-calf heifers in for the winter. They were strung out down a hollow seeking shelter from squally showers under the lee of a wood. There were 30 of them, quite big cattle, and to come towards the buildings where I needed them, they had to climb the bank, but Mert stuck to his task and eventually won the battle of wills. It took him 20 minutes, he was out of my sight much of the time, and it was as good a piece of work as he has ever done.

It triggered memories of Poppy, (I didn't give her that name) a quite remarkable bearded collie that I had, probably the best working dog I ever owned and for some reason, I remembered Smut. Smut was a little black bitch that I bought when she was three years old. I used to love Giles's cartoons in the *Express*; he sometimes drew a black collie dog, lying down, with just one eye showing. That was Smut. She used to lie like that in our back yard and should a visitor arrive, she would allow them to pass her by without any flicker of attention. It was in the actual act of knocking at the door that she would have slipped down the yard behind them, administered a sharp nip in the backside and be away back up the yard and round the corner out of sight. I bought her off a renowned sheepdog breeder who had paid a lot of money for her. He had bred her twice and at each pregnancy she had had just one large pup and not a litter. She had had to have a caesarean section to remove each pup and was therefore considered unsuitable for further breeding. It's an ill wind etc, so I acquired a very well-bred bitch for reasonable money.

But I couldn't get her to work. She settled in here very well, probably enjoying the attention she received as the sole dog on a farm rather than being just one of many. I'd take her into my field with sheep and she'd regard them like a coiled spring, just waiting to get around them. I'd look at her and she'd look at me and it was obvious that something was missing. I'd say 'get bye' or 'come bye' and nothing would happen, she might take a few tentative steps, but that was it. It was frustrating for me and clearly frustrating for her. It came to pass that there were some sheepdog training classes in our area so I booked Smut and I a place.

We had to go to a neighbouring farm where a ten-acre field had been set up with the hurdles and pen that you see on television at sheepdog trials. There were about ten of us there and we had to wait out turn to go out with our dogs and firstly tell the instructor something about our dogs and then try to put the sheep around the course.

When our turn came I took Smut out to the instructor, he was from North Wales, and I told him all about her. He knew how she was bred, who'd bred her and her history. 'You've only got one problem with this little bitch, Roger, she's Welsh-speaking. Do you mind if I try her out?' And he did, and off she went like a rocket, she put the sheep through the hurdles and into the pen without fault, even earning a round of applause from the onlookers. We never looked back, Smut and I, after that and had a working partnership that sadly only lasted a couple of years. She came with me down to the main road one day to post a letter and I think she was getting a bit deaf, she went a yard too far and her head was clipped by a lorry cutting a corner. Not a mark on her, but very dead.

Not to finish on a sad note, when we were at sheepdog classes, a neighbour took his dog forward to the instructor, told him about him and then sent him off around the sheep. The dog set off at a fairly casual trot towards the sheep, his tail wagging continually. He stopped twice on his journey to urinate on clumps of nettles, he eventually got to the sheep and equally casually moved them up the field, and he had a sort of control of them, which slipped away whenever he stopped to sniff at something. 'Call your dog back, David,' said the man. 'When a dog wags its tail, it's a conscious effort; it isn't like breathing for example, which is something that is done automatically, without any thought whatsoever. So when your dog wags its tail it's using its brain to tell its tail to wag, and I'm afraid that once your dog's brain has told its tail to wag, there is hardly any brain-power left for it to work sheep for example.' David wasn't best pleased with this appraisal of his dog.

The rest of us thought it was hilarious.

JANUARY 8TH 2011

There was a time in my life when I did quite a lot of shooting. Not posh expensive shooting, more a gang of sophisticated poachers who rented a small shoot and did all the gamekeeper work amongst themselves. It was always good fun, good company and with the added pleasure that comes from having a good working dog. But life moves on, mine did in particular, and I pulled out of shooting and had to decline invitations because there was no room in my diary. I suppose I've been shooting about four times in the last five or six years, and if the maxim 'practice makes perfect' is true, I'm no longer much of a shot. Last year I went out in January, I'd had a bad fall in December, couldn't lift my gun properly and had five shots and absolutely nothing to show for it.

I was invited to the same shoot again in December and we all know what December has been like. The due day when it came was dreadful and I did wonder if I needed to be out in such weather. I decided I didn't but it's bad manners not to turn up. But I did decide that if I had another day that was a repeat of last time, then it would be my last shooting day, ever.

But if you are going to do anything then you also have to give it your best shot, so I did. I shot five birds on the first drive with eight shots, which is quite good by most standards. I've never taken a shot at low birds and I didn't then. I enjoyed the day out and shot about average, amongst people who shoot once every week and some weeks several times. I know that many of you reading this will not condone shooting under any circumstances. It's important to me that all the game shot is eaten but there is another positive spin-off. The wood and coverts that are preserved for game shooting provide an environment for lots of other wildlife.

More importantly still, in the harsh weather, shooters feed pheasants, partridge and duck. This food, usually wheat, is also available to anything else that wants to eat it. So when you are standing cold and shivering at your appointed peg, waiting for the game birds to come over, you soon discover that you are amongst a host of other wild birds that shelter in those very same woods with ample food at hand. This may not in itself justify the shooting to many of you but if there was no shooting, the woods may or may not remain but no one will be putting out wheat there at £170 a ton!

★★★

Monday this week was our worst day thus far during the present freeze-up. I get no comfort from that because everything in life is relative and the next worst day will inevitably turn up. We were at -18°C which tested us. This is an understatement. Amongst all the big problems like thawing milking equipment out and getting water troughs to run, the biggest problem on that particular day was to get all the tractors running.

It was so cold that some tractors eventually started and then stopped again because the diesel was waxing up. It took us an hour and a half to get one particular and essential tractor going. I don't intend to catalogue all the hardships of farming in this sort of weather, but even the most simple jobs take two or three times as long to accomplish. Just be glad, if you eat food, that the people who manage roads railways and airports, don't do the farming!

But we do get going eventually and after lunch I set off to feed the dry cows. My slow journeys on tractors are an opportunity to observe what is going on in nature, all about me. I have a good clear view of the fields to my left because the door of this loader is missing. It's been missing for two years because it went away for new glass but that's another long story.

Every field I pass is pristine white with snow, but there is a difference today. Every field I pass has fresh molehills to show. Not just odd ones, veritable clusters of them, the freshly-turned soil showing starkly against the snow. You have to pause to consider just how remarkable this is. How on earth did this little animal manage to push all this fresh soil out? From how deep did the fresh soil come? And however did it push it up through the frozen ground? Remember I said it was -18°C that day, a day that comes at the end of a sequence of freezing days that goes back somewhere near a month. And if all that is not remarkable enough, why do all the moles apparently do it on the same day? Isn't nature amazing: is it any wonder that it fascinates us?

I won't use the word remarkable again although it's tempting, but by an amazing coincidence, the night before I'm in bed reading (I know that's a bit sad) and I'm reading a book written in 1887, it's about gamekeeping and poaching and along with that the reader gets a whole lot about nature. I'll quote directly from the piece I read. '*In a frost if you see a thrush on a molehill it is very likely to thaw shortly.*' '*Moles seem to feel the least changes in the temperature of the earth; if it slackens they begin to labour, and cast up, unwittingly, food for themselves!*' So it's a sort of explanation and something noted all those years ago. It is something I will note in future as a precursor to thaw. We didn't actually get a thaw, next day it was -2°C but that was 16° warmer than the day before and as I say, everything in life is relative; who is going to take a mole to task for being 2° out? Good luck to them, just keep off my lawn.

JANUARY 15TH 2011

We don't do broilers any more; we produce point-of-lay pullets for outdoor laying units. Some time ago, perhaps 18 months ago, three of these pullets escaped at loading time. They hung about the poultry sheds for a couple of weeks during which time the three became one, as the fox took his toll. This remaining pullet wisely moved away from the poultry sheds and went to live with the cows. To all intents and purposes, she became a cow. If you only have one calf, Farm Assurance will recommend you put in a mirror so that calf can see another calf even if it is itself.

The hen didn't have this sort of issue. It picked its food out of the cow ration. It went in to the collecting yard with the cows at milking time. It went through the parlour with the cows, I don't expect farm assurance recommends that. She roosted in the cubicles and seemed quite content with her life as a cow. You could tell from her bright red comb that she was laying and sometimes we would find some eggs.

When the spring came she would go off down the fields with the cows and come back with them at milking time, but wisely she always stayed around the yard after afternoon milking. In the winter we use a big square bale in the front of the loader to push the silage back to the cows, and the hen, who was mostly picking about amongst the silage, would get on the bale for a ride until I had finished.

But life is never as good as it seems and there is always a downside. The downside as far as the hen was concerned turned up in the shape of our corgi pup. The pup spends her whole day terrorising all our other livestock, mostly chasing cats, and the hen would have its share of rough treatment. One day it got a bit too rough so we don't have a hen any more. But the corgi shows every sign of becoming a good cow dog and as a friend of mine once said, 'I've never seen a good working dog yet, that hadn't killed a hen.'

It's all very well for a hen to think it's a cow. It's all very well for a hen to live the life of a cow. And as we know, foxes don't bother cows. But foxes can come in very different forms. I've got paperwork somewhere that says that I bought my wife a pedigree corgi pup for her birthday, it says that this pup is a pedigree corgi, but somewhere in the genes of this puppy, there is a good dose of fox and, I suspect, a touch of wolf.

★★★

On New Year's Eve I decide to go to the pub for a couple of hours. There's often good kissing to be had in the pub on New Year's Eve. I go at seven o'clock and when I arrive there are only two people in there, the landlord and my son, I'm certainly not inclined to kiss either of them but we'll see what happens. My son has to go at 7.30 because he's got to do evening milking. I have to go at 9.30 because I've got to get up at 3.30 for the early morning milking. As I drive home through the village people are making their way to the pub. It crosses my mind that my son and I have a full day's work in front of us next day, New Year's Day, and that most of the rest of the population will have a late start to the day. It crosses my mind that there are lots of dairy farmers in a similar position to us, struggling to make any money out of milk, working ridiculous hours. Why do we do it and for how much longer?

★★★

The really, really bad weather went away; really bad weather to us means double figure frosts. Then last Friday, as a sort of postscript, we had about six inches of snow. I quite like driving about in snow; actually, I think I'm quite good at it. I like driving off-road in it and I like driving around the unclassified roads around here, which, as we all know, saw less salt during the prolonged cold spell than a packet of salt and vinegar crisps.

I'm off as soon as it's light, about my business. First I go to see how many of my neighbour's sheep are (uninvited) in my field today. To be fair to the sheep, they have nothing to eat in their own field but to be fair to me, why should I keep them? There are about 30 there this morning, it's been three weeks now, and I can feel a nasty letter and a bill coming on. Next I go up to our other buildings to see the dry cows. It's quite a steep road but the 4x4 goes up it without any trouble.

When it's time to come back down I make sure I'm in four wheel drive and in the lowest gear and without much other thought, I let it make its own way down. About half way down and we're away: we just gather speed, faster and faster. It's a funny feeling being totally out of control and knowing there's nothing you can do. I manage to keep on the road, there's the option of a very steep drop on the right, but it could be curtains at the T-junction. In the few seconds I have, I work out that there is a car along here every ten minutes and life will surely send one along now. I shoot straight across the junction really fast, and go through the hedge on the other side. No cars, can't believe it! While I'm waiting to be pulled out, ten come by, and I wonder if they realise how lucky they have been. Me? I've always been lucky.

JANUARY 22ND 2011

In the pub there's much talk of shooting. A lot of those that sit in my corner are in local shoots. Not posh expensive shoots, more the 'do a bit of shooting, do a bit of beating' sort of shooting, and pay a share of the expenses. This brings shooting within the reach of those who would never even have dreamed of shooting a generation ago. So that's a good thing. They all have a love of wildlife which some of you may find perverse. There's a degree of urgency to their shooting talk lately because the remaining weeks of the season are slipping away at some speed.

Shooting, like most activities, has its share of anecdotes, such as the dry comment of a beater in the pub one night that a local titled lady, calling her dog back when it had gone too far in front, sounded very similar to the noises that a sow makes when it is stuck under a gate. There are a lot of expensive shoots in this area where guns are charged up to £45 a bird shot. Sometimes they book a 500-bird day and have to pay the price, even if they don't shoot that many. Work that out, divided in to eight guns! An expensive day out especially on a foul weather day.

A few years ago, when I was even more important than I am now, I was invited on one of these corporate days by a manufacturer of dairy equipment. We were invited to stay the night in a stately home the night before on the estate where the shoot was held. I wasn't sure what the form was so I took £100 with me. At breakfast we all had to guess how many birds would be shot in a sort of sweepstake. This cost £20 apiece. At lunch we were allowed to make a second guess for another £20. Throughout the day I had the services of a loader, who loaded and carried my gun and cartridges. I asked someone else on the shoot how much tip I was expected to give the loader, '£60'. Panic sets in. 'What about the head keeper, how much do I tip him?' 'Your host tips him.' There's lucky, my £100 was already gone!

They were talking in the pub about a party of French men that had been shooting on a nearby estate. There's a strict code of safety conduct that must be rigidly enforced in shooting, especially when you have beaters driving the game from in front of the guns. Ground game, - rabbits and hares - are usually safe on shooting days, because there needs to be complete safety for the humans, beyond what they are shooting at. Anyway on the first drive one of the Frenchmen shot at a very low bird and just one pellet hit a beater, but, dramatically it hit him on one of his front teeth, which was a cap and the tooth was knocked out. The beater thought it was hilarious and took it all in very good humour. I know I wouldn't have - after all, your mouth isn't that far away from your eye! Anyway the Frenchman passed over ample euros to pay for a new cap, sort of crossed his palm with silver, and they went on to the next drive. This was down a long valley hillside that was deep in bracken, all the beaters were clearly visible to the guns who were spaced out at the bottom. There were about ten beaters in the line, the man who had hit the beater was the first to raise his gun and as he did, almost as if there was an unseen signal the ten beaters disappeared in to the bracken.

JANUARY 29ᵀᴴ 2011

I was at a farmers' meeting in Cumbria yesterday, and a friend of mine, sitting next to me, had his hand heavily bandaged so inevitably I asked him what he'd done. He said he was milking and a freshly calved heifer had missed her footing in the parlour and ended up with one leg dangling down in the pit where the milker works. He'd had this happen before and was lifting her foot back up on to the standing so that she could get back up on to her feet. The heifer for her part, probably a bit scared, was trying to find somewhere secure to place this foot and in flailing her leg about to find a foothold, managed, inadvertently, to trap his hand between a metal part of the milking parlour and her hoof. The extra purchase put the heifer back on her feet but my friend had all the flesh stripped off the back of his hand. So graphic was the description that I wished I hadn't asked him: 68 stitches!

There's always a degree of one-upmanship abroad. A farmer the other side of the table had heard all this and told us his hand injury story. He had been handling some cows and had become trapped by a cow against some railings; in a desperate attempt to avoid being crushed and seriously injured he had punched the cow's head and had suffered a bad injury to his hand, an injury that subsequently required surgery. He was taken to hospital and there taken for treatment. In considerable pain he was taken aback at the uncaring attitude of the doctors and nurses. Instead of trying to nullify his pain and discomfort they seemed to go to great lengths to hurt him further. A big burly man, he said it got so bad that he was crying out in agony. A doctor asked him if it hurt, and the farmer said that he was close to passing out. 'Serves you right' said the doctor and proceeded to inflict further pain. Eventually the farmer couldn't cope anymore and called a halt to proceedings by threatening to hit the next person who touched his hand. 'What do you expect, why should we treat you with care?' 'What are you on about?' asks the farmer. 'Hitting your wife so hard you damaged your hand.' 'I didn't hit my wife, I hit a cow.' 'It says here you on your admissions notes you hit your wife.'

So he explained what had happened and within a few minutes he was nicely sedated and drifting painlessly away as they took him down for surgery. Seems that when he was admitted the message to the admissions desk had become 'he hit the cow'. The receptionist assumed that the cow was his wife. Which despite being an amusing story, also ends up as a commentary on life itself.

February 5ᵗʰ 2011

The nights are getting perceptibly lighter. Everyone remarks on it, as we all look for the harbingers of spring. The cornfields and grassland are greener than I expected they would be after the severe frosts. I've had dry cows and heifers outside most of the winter grazing turnips. They came in at night when the winter was at its worst, but when I drive by them they are always grazing contentedly. I give them silage every day to fill them up and to keep them full but I can tell that they are very content because they are not eating as much as I thought they would. So we inadvertently wish our lives away as we look forward to the spring, the best time of the year, and I have to order some fertiliser. Fertiliser prices are always linked to oil and gas prices! 'How much?' Will I have to get a security company to spread it for me?

Where we live, security has never been a big issue. We had some cash taken out of the house 18 months ago but as far as we know the farm equipment has been safe. There's a nagging doubt at the back of my mind because we can never find tools and equipment and if we can't find it, how do we know if we've still got it? And as the value of what we have about the farm increases, diesel and fertiliser for example, it becomes more attractive to steal. Our local village hall had the fuel tank emptied last week and the number of 'visitors' looking to buy scrap has increased. I tell those that work here to make a note of vehicle number plates if they are suspicious. That's probably a bit naive of me: who would go around stealing with authentic number plates? A farmer in Gloucestershire told me that if you really want to make them cross, take a picture of them next to their vehicle with a mobile phone. (Might get your barns burnt down, mind).

★★★

It was a big rugby day in our family a couple of weeks ago. My son, whose appearances on the rugby field are now mostly restricted to a second half appearance as a substitute, was to play his first game with his son, my eldest grandson Rhys, who is now 17 and old enough to play with the big boys. It's a bit of a family tradition, because I made my way down the sides as I got older and I met my son on his way up and we actually played in the same side for two years. He started playing when he was 15, which was allowed in those days. We even, my son and I, went on rugby tours together. We drank in different groups, but off-hand I don't remember us embarrassing each other. So how did father and son prepare for this important occasion?

Well my son had to do the midday milking before he could play rugby and my grandson had to help his dad with the milking so that they could finish in time to play. I was down at the rugby club at a lunch and know that when their teammates were warming up out on the field, father and son were probably washing the parlour out, 14 miles away. They were both there before kick-off, but only just.

Most farmers would like to see their sons follow them onto the farm. Some actively encourage their sons to make it happen, some just hope it secretly so as not to exert undue pressure. I'm sure my son is no exception. My grandson has not made any commitment to farming but has focused his sixth form lessons towards teaching P.E. But it must surely cross his mind that there is a lot of anti-social activity involved in the commitment to milking cows. It was suggested to me at the rugby club that I should get changed and make a five-minute appearance so that we could say that there were three generations on the field at the same time. *I can reassure you that what tiny bit of dignity I still have, is intact.*

★★★

One thing that I can't do with is people going on and on about their ailments. It's just a form of hypochondria, it's just attention-seeking. But have I told you about my bad shoulder? I'm sure I have. It's been a problem for over 12 months now and I've had enough of it. I've mentioned it to the doctor who never seems very interested. I gained some respite by going to a chiropractor, but it was £35 a go and as soon as I stopped going it went back to being a bad shoulder. It only bothers me when I'm asleep but sleep is very precious to dairy farmers. So I've started going swimming again to try to exercise it away. I used to do a lot of swimming, not very quick swimming but I could keep going for ages.

When they built our local pool, it was never pay-on-the-door, it was for organisations to hire by the hour. If you wanted to hire it for an hour you had to provide your own qualified life-saver! To make sure there was a nucleus of qualified life-savers, about 12 of us did the course. We all did our duties free. In the summer of 1976, a hot dry year that is etched in my memory because there was little to do on a dairy farm apart from watch the cows paddle about in dust and watch the fields burn, I did life-saver duty every single afternoon of the school holidays so that the children could have a swim. Do you think that you've ever had power like the power that decides when those with red wrist bands get out of the pool and the blues can get in?

For years I used to run the local youth club and we would hire the pool once a week. I would be the life-saver, I used to do it once a week for the local primary school as well, and I would take the children the five miles to the pool, with other parents. One day I turned up in the village with my own two children and there were eleven more waiting to go, but no parents. Dilemma. If I took half of them, who would look after their safety while I went back for the rest? Solution. Thirteen children in the car. I used to have an old Morris Oxford and I squeezed them into that. You just wouldn't dare do that these days!

So now we go to the over-50s swimming. I was disappointed that they didn't ask me to prove I was over 50! My shoulder hurts more but I might be doing it some good. It's all very interesting; I've never seen anything move as quick as women over 50 can, as they scurry from the changing room to the pool side to get their bodies out of sight and under the water. The women swim slowly up and down on one side of the pool, and the average men go up and down the other side. There are a few men who can swim quite fast but they go up and down with the women. This is called showing off. I go up and down with the women as well but that's because I'm the slowest swimmer there. I note, as I gather my breath, that all the life-savers have the same uniform and I have found out that they now get paid.

And another of life's cycle is completed. One of the life-savers is my grandson.

FEBRUARY 19TH 2011

There's a row of small bungalow-type dwellings in our village. Historically they have mostly housed retired agricultural workers and/or their wives, an ideal solution for anyone who retired, who had previously lived in a tied cottage. It brought them into the village centre to live out their retirement years, which they all seemed to relish, having often lived their working lives in isolated cottages on isolated farms. And it also solved the problem of freeing up the tied cottage for the next farm worker.

So this guy I've never seen before turns up in the pub one night, talking with an accent more 'Del boy' than anything around here. Inevitably I ask what's his name and where does he come from? Turns out he's from Hampstead, no connections in the area whatsoever, first time in fact he's been in the county. I've nothing against him personally, as long as he doesn't come and sit by me in the pub and start to talk about 'West 'am'. But I do ask of a parish councillor 'how come one of these dwellings was allocated to someone from so far away and wasn't there a local person needing it?' 'If one is vacant it has to be advertised nationally and he has as much right to it as anyone else.' So you have to ask, being a bit simple, what drives all that? 'It's his human rights.' So that's alright then.

★★★

I'm driving back from our rented buildings down a narrow lane and there's a lady who lives in a cottage nearby taking her dog for a walk. So I stop and wind the window down to say 'Hello' and pass the time of day. That's the sort of person I am. Warm and friendly, time in my life for anyone. It's a mistake. 'You made a hell of a mess of the road when you were carting slurry last week, I had a job to get up the hill when I came home from work and I had to wash the car next day.' This is all true. We carted slurry for two days, the first day the ground was frozen hard but it thawed the next day and as the frost came out of the ground the soil became very sticky and stuck to the wheels. We packed the job in because of the mess and we made a good job of cleaning it up with a rotary brush, but there were a couple of hours when it was, as she says, a hell of a mess.

But she's not finished yet. 'You've got a lot of rats up here.' Seems they are now my rats, by some sort of proxy on adoption. I think I'm on safer ground now. 'The keeper has caught over 100 now (101) and we are putting down poison three times a week so I think we are getting on top of them; I've got a problem with all the fencing debris up there which is the landlord's.' This is clever stuff, I've shared the rat population with the landlord at a stroke and she rents her cottage off the same landlord so she is less likely to make a fuss now. Not a bit of it. 'My dog came home with a dead rat and we had to take him to the vets in case he had ingested poison and we've got to watch him closely for three weeks.' This is more difficult than the slurry on the road. There are too many rats, true. But you can't poison them in case her dog finds one and if you can't poison them there will be even more rats and so you can't see an easy solution if you follow her logic, assuming there is a logic. Sometimes it's best to retreat, and I do. We've taken our very old Discovery off the road for the winter, if I'd been in that I wouldn't have had this trouble, because the windows don't wind down.

★★★

Stephen, who works for us, is feeding our replacement heifer calves. We built a new shed for them a couple of years ago. We built it ourselves and I thought we had made a fair job of it. We only rear our replacement dairy heifers in there, which allows us to clean it out and rest it before the next heifers start arriving. The shed is 60 feet by 30 feet with a snow mono-pitch roof, all clean and airy and open on one length facing the sun. There's only 12 calves in there now because the older ones have moved on to the next stage of the rearing process, 11 of these are weaned and there's one late heifer calf still on milk. Stephen says he looked up because he thought he heard the milk lorry coming up the yard, he thought it must be a big lorry because it was making more noise than usual.

It had been very windy here now for four or five days and it wasn't a lorry at all, it was a particularly violent gust of wind. He could track its progress because as it passed over a row of traditional buildings, he could see the slates being plucked off the roof. It seemed to pick the calf shed out deliberately. It took half the roof off in one bite. (I'm not sure if bite is the right description, we've all heard of a biting wind but that's meant to describe a cold wind).

It took this 30' x 30' piece of roof up in to the air without any effort and put it down 100 yards away in my neighbour's winter wheat field. It then took the next section, 30' x 15' about 30 feet up in the air, turned it over a couple of times to have a look at it and then put it back in what is now left of my shed. But not where it got it from, on its edge and about a step away from Stephen, who is taking a great interest in all this. He seemed mostly concerned about his own personal safety, while I was concerned that he hadn't tried to grab hold of the roof and hold it in place. It's difficult to get commitment these days.

The calves for their part think it's all great fun and there is much kicking up of heels and jumping into the next pen. So we now have just a quarter of the shed we had a few minutes ago and we have to do something with the calves. You will possibly remember that I'm always complaining that Nature never sends me enough heifer calves. That I need 40-50 a year but that I never get them. Well this year we've had 27. But I've got room for 40-50 elsewhere and so later that day we put the 11 older calves in the trailer and take them to join 13 slightly older calves in a nice big shed.

So we are left with just a couple of problems: we have to

recover the shed roof from the wheat field, we have to put it back on or possibly buy a new roof, and we have one little calf on its own. Under Farm Assurance, of which I am a great fan, a calf should always be able to see another calf. They will even advise you to put a mirror in the pen so it can see itself! I haven't got a spare mirror so for the time being this calf will have to imagine it's a cat or dog until another calf turns up.

February 26th 2011

Quite a lot of the old established farming families around here moved into the area in the depression years of the 1920s and 30s from the mid-Wales counties of Montgomeryshire and Radnorshire. I suppose they are three or four generations down that particular journey in life now, but it's a phenomenon that has always intrigued me. They must have been a very special breed of people, when all about them was despair, unemployment and failure, to put themselves in a position to better themselves by moving down to larger lowland farms. Both sides of my wife's grandparents made this journey and I remember her father telling me that when they moved to Shropshire, they had the choice of six farms that they could have rented. It still wasn't easy; it would be hand-to-mouth stuff for years to come. They would eat what they could grow, and the power on the land had to be grown, in the shape of horses, the rent was paid with sales of rabbits, but survive they did and most of them flourished. It's a story of great fortitude and courage and pride, but there's one factor of the phenomena that has always intrigued me. Just as soon as they had made the move, they considered themselves to be English. It must have been important for them to wholly embrace where they had moved to and what they had become. It's something that still resonates today when immigrants to the UK from around the world are sometimes accused of not actually making that sort of step. That's not a topic on which I want to elaborate.

★★★

Our one full-time employee retired just after Christmas and last summer we had the opportunity to employ someone to replace him, with someone I've known for years and years and it was too good a chance to miss. It's worked well, we've always treated our employees as one of the family, we never tell them to do things, we ask them, and we never ask them to do something we are not prepared to do ourselves. I know it's worked well for him because we've got mutual friends who tell us so. He turned up every day over Christmas in that freezing weather although we didn't ask him but those two or three hours every day made such a difference. Likewise, if he wants the odd day off in the week to go to something special, then he can have it, it's no big deal. When my wife's mother and father moved down here all those years ago, they brought some staff with them. Two of them were the grandparents of Stephen, who works for us now. I think that's a nice story.

★★★

Come the first nice, spring-like Sunday and our world and everyone else's world, and our roads in particular, will be full once again with motorbikes. These high-powered machines that go too fast for the people who ride them, who apparently, under their helmets, are mostly middle-aged men reliving their youth on the expensive high-powered machines that they couldn't previously afford. Sadly there will be reports in the Monday evening papers of crashes and fatalities. But we've had motorbikes in the winter this year. The lane up to our farm is a council road and after the farmyard it goes to the next village but it's been 'let go'– you can only get through with a 4x4, tractor or motorbike.

There's a bit of me that resents traffic on this road: it's a sort of backdoor to our yard with possible security issues. They come mostly on Sundays and you can hear them coming in the distance.

They are sort of off-road bikes, road legal but what I would call motor-cross. There are usually about 20 of them and they come at ten-yard intervals, sounding like angry wasps. I enjoy driving off-road and must stop begrudging them their pleasure. I watch them come through the yard.

The last one's got a bit of a wobble on. There's a sheepdog biting lumps off his front wheel and a corgi dragging along in the mud with a goodly mouthful of his leggings. I feel a damaged bike claim coming along.

Spring

MARCH 5TH 2011

On an agricultural front, I'm getting a bit twitchy. I've never known our land to be so soft and wet and yielding. I'm sure it's something to do with the frost coming out of the ground that has made it like it is. Meanwhile the work is just piling up. You can look over the gate at what needs to be done but you just daren't take a tractor into the field to do it. We grow most of our first cut silage with poultry manure which, given the price of fertiliser this year, is the agricultural equivalent of gold dust. This is usually spread by now, but the heaps are sitting in the fields as a constant reminder of how far we are behind.

We have lots of farmyard manure to spread and plough in and spring wheat to sow. By now we have usually put some fertiliser on the cow-grazing area, in fact in some years we've had the cows out in the daytime by now. The only thing that I can imagine drying the land up quickly is a cold east wind, but we don't particularly want that either. At the back of my mind I know that the work will get done, it always does, but that doesn't stop me getting twitchy.

I'm at a meeting: the agenda is not too testing, so I'm looking about me, as is my custom. I focus on the man opposite me. He has, thus far, made a big contribution to the meeting, bigger than mine, I haven't had a lot to say thus far, he's done a lot of talking but he hasn't got a lot to say either, if you get my drift. Trouble is, he doesn't know that. He keeps on stating the obvious and repeating what others have already said, neither of which I have ever seen much point in. To be fair, he looks the part; he's better turned out than me. He's got one of those coloured shirts on with a white collar. I've always wanted one of those but it wouldn't be practical, given the state of my neck. He's got on a very tasteful tie, and I can tell his suit cost a shed-load of money compared with mine.

I push my chair back nonchalantly to have a look under the table at his shoes. Oh joy! They are filthy. He obviously hasn't cleaned them for ages. What a let-down! What double standards! I might not be as well or expensively dressed, but I always clean my shoes. For reassurance I glance down to look at my own feet. I'm appalled, although I know that I cleaned them this morning: they are muddy and dusty, and if anything, worse than those of the man opposite. I can't get over it; it's just not like me to go out with dirty shoes.

When I get home I investigate how my shoes got so dirty. The ten yards between the kitchen door and where I park my car is reasonably clean. There's some corgi poo, been there a week now, but I know where it is and have obviously avoided it, as it is, shall we say, undisturbed, if that isn't too much information. Then it dawns on me. I open the car door and on the floor on the driver's side is several weeks' accumulation of dried mud, dried cow muck and other debris. Some use cleaning your shoes to go out if they are going to get filthy in the vehicle you go out in.

★★★

I've told you that I think it's important to support the pub in the village, lest it should go the way of so many others, and close its doors. The countryside abounds with closed pubs and closed garages. Unfortunately their demise can be placed squarely on the shoulders of the supermarkets. In fact, I've been working on occasions in rural areas that I'm not familiar with, and driven miles looking for fuel, past lots of closed garages, and inevitably ended up at a supermarket fuel pump. As part of our pub support, there's a group of us, 25 or so, that meet once a month for a meal. We call it fine dining, but it's very informal and the idea is that our main course is a traditional local dish. The first time we met we had what is called Fidget pie, which was largely ham and apple. Last night we had a memorable meal of mutton, really superb, followed by wimberry pie, a locally-sourced berry that was also really excellent. Inevitably conversation drifts towards what we will have to eat next month. It looks as though it will be a pork and port casserole.

But there are other suggestions. Someone suggests that we should have rabbit; half the people there reckon they've not eaten rabbit since 'myxy' and don't intend to start now. So that's a non-starter. Someone else wants us to have grey squirrel. None of the women say they will come to eat that. There's an argument about it. Can't say I fancy it myself but I don't really know why. The only plus that I can see is that if the women didn't go, well all the men would save the tenner that the meal costs.

MARCH 19TH 2011

As usual, there's one eye on what is in front of me on the tractor and there's one eye that scans the horizon and all that is to be seen between me and all the other fields that roll out to that horizon. I can see who is doing what in which field. I can see fertiliser going onto land, I can see ewes and lambs and I can see the numbers of those sheep increasing daily as more ewes lamb indoors and they and their lambs are transferred outside. 'What's that?' Something fresh catches my eye. 'How long have they had black sheep?'

I can see, in the far distance, these black shapes moving over a grass field. It's worth a better look, so I stop the tractor at the end of the field and open the door. If I don't have to look through the window, I get a much clearer view, take my word for it. There are eight black shapes and I can see now that they are turkeys. I'd heard that there were some wild turkeys on the next-door estate and now they have strayed closer to our ground. I hope they do that more often; I've missed the turkeys being about. I used to enjoy turkey spotting with my grandchildren on Sunday afternoons in the summer.

★★★

We use quite a lot of gas here (LPG). There are two big tanks for the poultry sheds, a tank of gas for vehicles and a tank for the central heating in the house. The central heating was justified by the bed and breakfast side of our business and comes as a sort of comfortable bonus. So the gas man, as they say, cometh, to renew our contract, and I take the opportunity to tell him that we ran out of gas for the house on 2nd of December and it took nine days to get some more. I remind him that we never ever normally order gas, that they always keep the tanks topped up automatically, that I spent half an hour a day on the phone listening to 'gas music' for nearly a week before anyone answered the phone and that the weather in December was bloody cold.

Warming to my task, which must be some sort of pun, I tell him that because we have gas, we only have as a reserve, an old oil fired cooker in the kitchen, which is so powerful that it will just, but only just, fry an egg for breakfast, providing you put the egg on before milking, and it will be ready a couple of hours later, (as long as you don't like your egg too well done). I explain that the warmish kitchen is about a day's walk from my bedroom and the heat from the one doesn't reach the other. We do have a single bar electric fire but, as we all know, dairy farmers can't afford those sorts of luxuries. All in all, I tell him, being without gas was a bit of a bugger. 'December,' he says: 'You were lucky, a refinery broke down, some of our competitors left their customers without gas for weeks.'

He launches in to more of the same sort of excuses which are designed to make me feel grateful for being cold for nine days. He's so good at it, the excuses, that I wonder if he might have been an agricultural contractor in a previous life. He avoids the bit about no one answering the phone for a week, but that's a minor detail. So we move onto the contract and get all signed up again, then he tells me he needs to see our tanks because, under new legislation, I will probably need new pipework underground. I ask him if this will be free, knowing the answer before I ask. So we go out of the kitchen and the first tank we inspect is the house tank. He looks at the pipework, and says it's OK. 'You're lucky,' he says: 'This tank has GPS.' 'What does that mean?' I know what it means and I can see where this is headed. I like it when people think that they can patronise me, there's usually good sport to be had. He quickly launches in to his patter about satellites and technology, spelling it all out as simply as he can, after all I am a simple farmer. 'To put it in a nutshell,' he says 'GPS will tell us in the office how much gas is in the tank so that we can fill it up without you having to read the dial and phone with an order.' This sentence comes out slower and slower as his voice tails off and it dawns on him just what it is he is saying, but it's part of his sales jargon and he can't stop himself. Gas man 0. Simple farmer 1.

★★★

Today, I would like to attempt to address the three issues of morality and promiscuity and practicalities. It's all part of my honesty, my determination to bring to your attention all that occurs about me in my daily life. So we have a sheepdog called Mert who is an important part of my life and I know that many of you like to hear about Mert because if I meet you, it's Mert that you ask about. Never mind how I am, (but that's life). Mert's had a difficult six months because his life has been plagued by a corgi pup who terrorises his every waking moment. How, for example, would you like to spend 10-15 hours every day with a corgi pup hanging off your ear? The corgi pup is a bitch pup. I sometimes think that there's more vixen in her than corgi and that it could be an issue for trading standards but we'll let that lie for now. The more perceptive of you will have worked out by now that as the corgi pup grows up, there could be problems. My wife flagged it up first, 'You'll have to get that dog castrated.' How could I do that? It would be like cutting my right arm off, or even worse! 'He's too big and she's too small.' A grunt in response. 'And Mert wouldn't do that, he's not that sort of dog.' Two grunts at this. Well, time passes and seasons come and go. Turns out the corgi is a tart, Mert is no better than he should be, they are both very practical when it comes to arrangements and I'm afraid they have.

MARCH 12ᵀᴴ 2011

I'm rolling grass on our high land. I stop the tractor and get off to stretch my legs. Actually I get off for a pee and Mert does likewise. I take a moment to survey the scene, something I never tire of doing. Above me somewhere I can hear skylarks, I can't see them because I haven't brought my glasses with me. I spend half my life trying to locate them in the house, so why would I bring them outside with me? As my eyes adjust to a longer distance I can see buzzards spiralling together. They must be pairing up and sorting out territories because there is a lot of activity within the group as they swirl about. I count 16 altogether. What chance of rearing a family of skylarks with that lot in close vicinity?

★★★

In the pub, the talk has moved quickly on from shooting to lambing. I like sheep but haven't had any for years, so I'm not much of a contributor to the lambing conversation but don't feel left out. Sheep and keeping sheep are not on the cards at all for this family. In fact, should I turn up at home with a trailer-load of sheep, my son would help me to unload them, but he would be gone next morning. Lambing can be a rollercoaster ride of triumphs and disasters and I don't need the disaster element in my life anymore.

I don't need the long hours. I used to find it easier to go out in the early hours if I was already fully dressed so I used to sleep on the settee for a month. I don't need go around shaped like a settee anymore. I didn't used to smell very sweet either! Life would revolve around the lambing shed, all day and much of the night and then, suddenly, it would all be over, probably after five or six weeks. I always thought there was strangeness to it all. So much effort and activity and then nothing. Just the debris and emptiness, perhaps the last dead lamb slung over a gate still to be disposed of.

***

It's little wonder that after all this effort to get the lambs born, that shepherds have such little patience for the predators that will prey on them as they move on to the next stage of their journey, from the lambing shed to the fields. The fox is usually chief amongst these. I lost 20 lambs one year to a vixen with cubs in an adjoining wood. I lost six lambs off some yearling ewes in the field next to our house to a badger, whose tell-tale sign is to open up the rib cage, as neatly as if you had done it with secateurs, as it searches to eat the organs.

'People' will write to newspapers and say that predators will only attack weak and sickly lambs that would probably die anyway, the fact that they are weak and sickly seeming to imply some degree of neglect by the farmer. These people have one thing in common; they've never kept sheep or done any lambing.

★★★

It's commonplace for my friends in the pub to have their ewes scanned to see how many lambs they are carrying. Those that are carrying just one lamb are frequently allowed to lamb outside because it is reasonable to expect that in the vast majority of cases, things will proceed safely. The biggest problems with this practice around here at the moment are the activities of ravens. Lambs are attacked when they are only partially born. Particularly distressing is the removal of the lamb's tongue, which makes it impossible for the lamb to suckle and it will inevitably die. The lamb that has lost both eyes to the raven will invariably survive.

MARCH 26ᵀᴴ 2011

It's been a cold dry week thus far and the tell-tale signs of spring are emerging, slowly, but emerging they are. The birds are certainly busy, especially the rooks. It's all too easy to get carried away by all this but we have a May fair around here in the first week of that month and many is the time I have stood at the fair, wet and cold, waiting for the children to have had enough and come home. The hills around the area have been white over with snow so I know full well that there is still plenty of time for some 'weather'. But, not overdoing it, I have been turning a few cattle out. Just a few here and there.

For Mert and I this is an important step along the seasonal route. For us it's time to get in the 4x4 and drive around these cattle every day. It's quality time together. The corgi is not part of these journeys just yet. I've had her in the truck but thus far she doesn't like it. Mert needs time away from her. He is what my eldest grandchildren would describe as 'loved up' at the moment. He stands in the back there now in a sort of trance, but time will take care of that and I'm sure it won't be long until he's terrorising passers-by again.

I am confident that the corgi will eventually prove a valuable addition to our team. She is aggressive to a high degree and I can't wait for them to be barking and growling at joggers and cyclists as we journey about. So it's quite a special moment for me as I open the gate into the succession of small fields where we run our dry cows and in-calf heifers. It's a narrow valley to start with and these cattle are at the top end in a hollow with woods on three sides, grazing contentedly out of the cold wind. I count them: 22. They are all in calf and if one were to calve earlier than you think, there's a fair chance she will be off on her own somewhere. They are all present and correct but one of the real purposes of these inspections is to check on progress before calving. There's a cow and a heifer that have started to 'alter' and need to come home before the weekend.

That's the important work done but I notice one cow looking over the fence towards the wood, her ears forward. Obviously something has made her curious. I pull up alongside her to have a look. There, five yards away in the undergrowth, is a very fine turkey stag. He's on full display as he fluffs his feathers out for the benefit of the cow. I often think there is a resemblance between a turkey display and that of a galleon under full sail.

Next morning, as soon as it's light, I repeat my journey. It's just nagging at me that the cow could calve before we take her home later in the day. The cattle have moved up a steep bank onto the next level of these fields and there, sure enough, in a corner by the hedge is the cow with her calf lying contentedly beside her. But it's not just cattle that I scrutinise on these journeys. Are there any hares about? There's some tussocky grass left from the winter and there's usually been a hare lying here. I drive slowly towards where I think she might be and there sure enough within five yards is that hare and she gets up and skips away through the hedge.

Our tractor driver was up on this field yesterday and he reported two foxes 'mousing' in the grass. They took no notice of him, confirming what the local gamekeepers are saying, that there has been a fresh load of urban foxes dropped off in the area. I drive only a couple of hundred yards and sure enough there is a fox.

You can almost tell the difference immediately between an urban fox and a 'local', in both appearance and behaviour. This fox has a mangey look about him, nothing sleek, he does go to the wood, but he strolls there; a wild local fox would be gone just as fast as he could go, but this one stops a couple of times to have a look at me. So I'm looking at the fox, the fox is looking at me. Mert looks at the fox and instead of growling like he usually does, he whimpers and wags his tail (foxes look like corgis and vice versa). We, in turn, are also being watched because out from under an oak tree in the hedge, comes the stag turkey, intent on chasing us all off.

★★★

I don't know quite how we got to rural populations in the pub. I think it must have been because our local school is up for closure under spending cuts. This always seems to be a sort of self-fulfilling prophecy to me, because if a school is threatened with closure, parents tend to avoid sending their children there, lest they have the upheaval of having to change schools in twelve months' time. So numbers fall and local politicians can say, 'I told you so'.

Then the conversation moved on to the subject of the many tiny cottages that there used to be where people reared large families. Many of these cottages are long gone now, their stone plundered, those that didn't fall down were refurbished and are used as holiday homes or they house newcomers who have retired around here. Neither category of which provide children for local schools. So then we have a competition about who can recall the largest family reared in a small cottage.

As usual there's always somebody who will beat you all hands down. 'I can remember those Jones who lived in a cottage up in the woods near us.' 'It was only two up and two down but they reared 14 kids there.' 'By God it was hard on them, no electric, no running water; he worked for the council and only got about £8 a week.' 'In the autumn you couldn't find a hazelnut or blackberry in any hedge within five miles of their cottage.'

April 2ND 2011

Over the last week or so I have rolled the farm. It's a job I like. It takes you, yard by yard, over the whole farm and gives you a good look at grassland and cereal crops and how they have come through the winter. I also like it because my son-in-law has a very wide set of rolls and I borrow these and the job is soon done. To the passer-by it may look a slow, repetitive job, endlessly up and down the fields, but like most jobs that have to be done, you can make of it what you will. It doesn't look very exciting, but driving on the M6 in the rush hour when it's raining can be exciting, and who wants to be excited like that? On grass fields for example, I go back and forward leaving successions of lovely dark and shiny stripes, like you get on a well-cut lawn. It looks really nice, it doesn't make a scrap of difference to the crops but it makes a big difference when the landlord drives by, as he surely will, and he sees how nice it looks as well.

Then there's the wildlife. My main concern is to do the rolling before the skylarks have laid their eggs but the ground is very firm and I did find one nest with two eggs that had survived the passage of the roller intact. You need to keep your eyes peeled for the wildlife: hares for example, slip quietly away, mostly behind your back, as they hear the approach of the tractor. In a grass field, a brown shape scuttles away close to the ground, my first sighting of a leveret this year and I am surprised at how well grown it is.

Next day, in a different field, I come across a dead hare. It's a fully-grown animal and I get off to look at it. I can't make out how it has died, the carrion crows have pecked a hole in its belly but other than that it is unmarked. It seems a strange death and it concerns me. Birds come to visit you, they probably don't know what you are doing, but they come to check anyway, to see if you have disturbed anything as you pass by. A red kite drops down about 20 yards away and watches me for about 20 minutes.

I see these birds every day now, whereas ten years ago its visit would have been remarkable. In another field, bordered by a stream there are a lot of wagtails around the boundary. These fly out of the hedge one after the other right up to the tractor. A couple of times they seem to disappear under the front wheel, so close do they get. I do an emergency stop on each occasion and the little birds are unscathed and it is then that I realise what they are about. They are protecting their territory against an intruder and actually attacking the tractor: they've got more bottle than me.

There's quite a lot of discussion on rolling in the pub (which sounds a bit sad). There's one school of thought that says you should roll very, very slowly, like road rollers do, because the weight of the roller is on the ground for longer. The other view is that you should roll quite quickly, the reason being that if something is sticking up more than it should be, like a stone for example, if you have a bit of speed about you, your momentum will give the offending object a harder clout and push it down out of the way. I don't have strong views either way: rolling for me comes like most of my views on life, a middle-of-the-road balanced view. In the case of rolling, my speed is determined by a different factor altogether, because the front throttle on my tractor is where the dog lies and I can only open up the throttle as far as his leg, which just happens to be an eminently sensible speed to go rolling.

My mobile rings; handy things, mobiles, on farms. I tried to change television programme last night with my mobile phone, it didn't work, but apart from that they are very handy. It's Stephen who works for us; he's ploughing a field half a mile away. He's stopped by the side of the road to eat his dinner but now the tractor won't go. Too much electronics on tractors. Our oldest tractor doesn't do electronics, and if it breaks down you can usually fix it with a spanner and a big hammer. More modern tractors have a little plastic lever on them, about the size of the indicator lever on your car. You start the engine, put it in gear and then you move this little lever forward or back according to which way you want to travel. So there he is with a 150HP engine that not will start, five furrows on the back, eager to plough, and somewhere a piece of plastic called a solenoid that will not send the right instructions and which for obvious reasons you can't hit with a hammer. So I make phone calls and the dealer has to locate a part, come out and fit it and he's sitting there for nearly four hours before he's away again. He thinks he's got problems: I can't get Radio Two on my tractor.

★★★

Life doesn't get much better than this, a beautiful sunny spring morning, up early, two cups of tea, (the first one with some sugar) and a drive around the cattle that are turned out. They are on the very top field, the extent of their run, but on the way I come across a hen turkey. I've not seen her before, but I've not seen the turkey stag I mentioned, for two weeks now. Up on the top field amongst the cattle, I notice that a rail has come off the fence next to the woodland. I go to fix it back on with some Farmer's Glory (bale string). Down below me in the wood I can hear the stag turkey calling out in his distinctive 'gobble'. I phone the keeper to tell him that there are now two turkeys about; I like to think that I am his eyes and ears when he's not about, just as he's mine.

I sometimes get an early morning text, 'Cow calved on your top field: both OK.' I tell him about the dead hare that I found back at home, and he tells me he has found five in the last few days, in poor condition. It's worrying, some virus going around the area? On my way home I find the stag turkey has found the hen and they are doing what turkeys do when they are in love. He breaks off to attack the truck as we drive by. He's a fearsome sight, and Mert and I are lucky to get away with our lives.

APRIL 9TH 2011

I don't know if there were a lot of shooting days cancelled during the winter because of the exceptional weather, I suspect that to be the case. Either way, there seem to be lots of pheasants about, a lot more than is usual. And in proportion to that, so too is the carnage of pheasants on the roads. At the moment it's nearly all cock pheasants. They stand splendidly in the middle of the road. What they are saying is, 'This B road, or at least 20-30 yards each side of it where I am standing, and in to the middle just as far as the white line, is mine.' And stand they do. I've not run one over yet but I've seen plenty stand firm and sometimes even move into the path of a vehicle trying to avoid them as they seek to protect their territory. Sometimes a driver in a line of traffic, with vehicles approaching from the other direction, has little room to manoeuvre and the fatality that occurs is almost inevitable. Next to be run-over will be the hen pheasants that the cocks are protecting - they are at present laying eggs. They will get off their nests once a day in a sort of torpor and wander out into the road and that will be that. It just seems such a waste and such a shame.

★★★

Our naughty promiscuous corgi has to go to the vets for an injection. This was always going to be an adventure. Our corgi is a free spirit. She has neither collar nor lead and to take her to a vet's waiting room was always going to be interesting. Our farm vets don't 'do' dogs and cats so we have to go to vets where we are not well-known. To start off, she doesn't like car travel yet so knowing that I can catch her and put her in the truck is not necessarily any consolation because getting her out will be tricky without her escaping and I know that if she escapes I won't catch her again. Eventually we manage to put her in a box. She's not best pleased. I manage to get her in the box but once there, she plans to escape.

My next worry had been her behaviour with other pets in the queue but there's only one other dog there, a greyhound. He's an old dog and I assume he's a rescued greyhound. He probably needed rescuing because he doesn't look as if he ever won anything. I've often thought that it would be a nice thing to do, to rescue a greyhound. But the ones I've come across always seem to have no spark to them, and this one is no exception. The action of a corgi destroying a box, from the inside, only merits from the greyhound a casual turn of the head and just a touch of a raised eyebrow.

It's our turn now and in we go. The vet says we have to weigh the corgi to get the volume of the injection right. I put her on their platform scales and loose her and she stands there as good as gold. Then it's payback time: she does one of the biggest number 2s I've ever seen a dog do. I hold her for her injection and that's it. The vet says to bring her back for another tomorrow but I know that vets are like dentists and doctors, they like the better things in life, so I say that if she gives me the injection, I'll do it myself. That didn't go down too well.

★★★

Never been that interested in statistics myself. They can be manipulated to mean anything. But here's a hard fact: a wild North American turkey stag can run at 20mph for 100 yards after any 4x4 truck that invades its space. This is not just a one-off. They will do it every day. I think this particular wild turkey could get further than that but he apparently thinks that 100 yards is sufficient distance to remove an intruder from his territory.

★★★

Nobody likes rats. Nobody I know anyway. Keeping rat numbers down is not easy; it's close to trying to stop the tide coming in, in its scale of difficulty. We have a rat problem on the farm we rent. The landlord lives there so he has a rat problem as well which he defines as mine that I have gifted to him. So we're having a bit of a rat purge and a part of this has been reducing rat-nesting possibilities. There's a 20 yards by ten yards patch near the yard that is overrun with brambles and four or five small thorn trees. While the leaves are off the briars you can see lots of rat holes in the ground. I often see buzzards perched on the fence, and I'm sure they can see the rats there but can't get at them because of the undergrowth. So one dry day we put a big bale of straw in the straw chopper and blast the straw all over the briars and apply a match. And a very fine blaze we have too. All the undergrowth is burnt up and all we have left are singed thorn trees.

Then I put my main man to cut the trees down so that in future the patch will be clear and less of a rat sanctuary. So he starts the chain saw up and just behind him out pops a rat. He doesn't like rats so he's off like a flash. But this is no ordinary rat; its fur is on fire. I'm sure that rats have feelings and suffer pain like the rest of us. But if I'm honest there's not a lot of concern about the rat. Until, that is, he heads off towards the bays of straw that are still full. Then we are all after him. Thankfully for the straw and the rat, his personal little fire is out before he gets there.

April 16ᵀᴴ 2011

This is a sad tale, and just as sadly, true. There was an old adage that a farmer's boy, or a boy on a farm, needed about his person: some string to tie, a knife to cut, and a shilling in his pocket for any eventuality. I'm not a boy any more but I'm still a boy at heart and there's a lot of merit in that old adage. It needs up-dating a bit, and I don't always have string in my pocket but there's always string in the tractors and farm vehicles, in fact there's mostly string about here everywhere (to my disappointment). I once experimented and dropped a piece of string against a wall on the yard. Everyone who went by during the next week must have thought, 'That's a handy place to drop some string', so a week later there was a veritable pile of string. It is serious if you don't have a knife in your pocket and I always double-check this before I leave the house. If I lose a knife outside, I agonise over where I used it last and nine times out of ten I remember, retrace my steps and find it. A shilling wouldn't be much use these days but there's usually a fiver in my back pocket. It's often a nice clean fiver as it's probably been through the washing machine with my trousers a couple of times, but if the occasion demands it can be carefully unfolded and pressed into service. If I were still a boy I would probably prefer to have enough money with me for a Travelodge in case my luck changed.

So I do have the farmer's boy of yesteryear's full kit. I add to that a pocket notebook and a broken pencil. I see things as I go about and I think of things when I'm on a tractor all day and I stop at the end of the field and write down a few words as a reminder. Thus when I get up early and write to you with these notes, I usually have enough of these reminders to make up an article. But then there's shirts and mobile phones.

In a survey of farmers a year or so ago, the mobile phone came out on top as the most useful modern invention on a farm. I could write article after article on how handy it is. You remember you need a load of diesel when you're away from the house and it's ordered just like that. You have a puncture in a field and you phone the tyre man. When my truck ran away down a hill in the snow and I went across a road and got wedged in a hedge, I couldn't open the doors to get out, so I just phoned for a tractor and chain: how handy was that?

Then there's shirts. The handiest place for me to carry a mobile phone in is the breast pocket of my shirt. Most of the year I wear a pullover on top and that helps to keep the phone safe. But some shirts don't have breast pockets and you can get caught out by the reflex action that stuffs your phone inside your pullover and into a pocket that isn't there. Usually it isn't very long before the phone pops out lower down and you have to put it in your trouser pocket. I did this last week and the phone popped out again within seconds. Unfortunately I was standing in front of the toilet and that's where the phone ended up. I retrieved it immediately, tried to dry it with tissue, but it wouldn't work. I split it up a bit and put it on the Rayburn for 24 hours. This dried it out nicely and it worked again but there was nothing to be seen on the screen. Which isn't very handy. So eventually I get a new phone and transfer the SIM card and it's all working OK. But now, finally and eventually, we get to the sad bit.

There was one of these boy bands rented a house in our village last winter for a New Year break. They were in the pub on and off for three days. They like it around here because they say the locals don't give them a hard time. They'll ask them if they can have a photo taken with them and that sort of stuff but after that they are left alone to mix in with everyone else and do their own thing. Now it so happens that one of these boys has a girlfriend who is by some distance the prettiest actress on Coronation Street and it also happens that I'm sitting on the settle in the pub and I happen to say to the person sitting next to me just how pretty she is and they go off and tell her what I've said and the next thing she's sitting on my knee and there's a photo of us on my mobile phone. I was telling someone this story much as I've told it to you and with one of my flourishes I pull out the phone to show them. But sadly she's no longer there; she's gone down the toilet.

★★★

There's some strange farmers in the pub. I know, all farmers are probably strange; these are different farmers then, not our usual farmers. One of them is sitting in my seat and I send an occasional scowl in his direction. There's been some summer grazing to let, just down the road, and they've come into the pub for a pint on the way home. They are what I call livestock farmers, having both sheep and cattle, but it's sheep that they live for. It's sheep that drive them and drive their lives. Because sheep are so important to them, they indulge in a sort of one-upmanship that seeks to establish themselves as really top-notch sheep farmers. 'Boy we've had some lambs this time.' 'And we have, we've cropped at 160%.' This is a mistake, to be so definitive, because another one comes back as quick as a flash: 'We've got about 180% this time.'

This beats the previous speaker and sets him back a bit. There's only the man who says he has 180% actually knows if this is true, there's no way of proving it either way. It could easily be a lie and probably is. So they drift into how many ewes have had triplets, not so much bragging now because too many triplets can be a nuisance. 'I had a ewe bring five lambs this time..' I bet he did. When I kept sheep I had a ewe thought she'd had six until I got four of them back to their right mothers. Now we're onto dogs. 'I've got a young bitch by Winston's Caps; boy is she coming on well.' This is how they talk about working dogs, the first name is the dog owner and the second the actual dog. The names of the owners are revered as top-class sheepdog trialists and to get a pup out of these top-class dogs is point-scoring at its highest. 'I've got a good bitch out of Cropper's Moss, best bitch we've ever had.'

The man who only had 160% last crop is still sulking so they try to mollify him and bring him back into the conversation. 'That's a good dog you've got Jim, who's he by?' 'He's by himself out in the Land Rover.' Worth going to the pub for little gems like that.

April 23ᴿᴰ 2011

A few weeks ago two of us here spent a long week of long hours on tractors, spreading muck, ploughing fields, working down the land and sowing spring corn. We pushed on hard for the week because it was dry and no one knows when the weather will break. We rolled the fields after sowing and left them tidy. But it didn't rain, not for some time, and the fields stood there for day after day, empty and bare. Then two nights ago we had some rain and next morning, on my rounds I can see the green shoots of the crops emerging in their uniform rows. Isn't it all wonderful!

★★★

My brother has a lovely house and a large garden. It didn't get like that by accident, it started out as a tiny cottage and a wilderness, it only got as it is now with a lifetime of hard work. The feature that makes the garden for me is the watercourse that runs right across it. It's bigger than a stream but it isn't quite a river, so we'll call it a brook. If his property were to feature on 'Escape to the Country' the compere of the show would point out the features of the garden and say 'and the river is yours'. For purposes of selling he would opt for the larger description, makes it look better value for money. But the river wouldn't be yours: you might own the ground either side of it, as my brother does, you might, for all I know, own the bed of the brook, but the water will never be yours, because all the water belongs to the Environment Agency.

There's a story about an officer from the Environment Agency (EA) who turned up on a farm and told the farmer that he was there to do an audit of their water usage. The farmer was bemused. 'We have our own spring for the farm buildings and we are on the mains in the rest, so we pay for that water.' But the EA man tells him that the water in the spring is theirs too and that will be part of the audit. As an example, he points to the pond in the middle of the yard, 'that's your pond but the water in it is ours, I will have to make a small charge for those ducks swimming on the pond on our water of say 25p per duck per week, that's ten ducks that's £2.50 a week.' The farmer is amazed at this and even more amazed when the inspector says that they must walk the whole farm to assess any other water usage. In the first field are the milking cows; it's a lovely field sloping down gently to a river in the valley with a fine herd of black and white cows taking their ease in the sun. The two men wander down to the river where some of the cows are having a drink. 'A milking cow will drink up to 10 gallons of water a day out of this river, I will have to charge you a £1 a day per cow for that. I counted 120 cows as we walked down the field, so that's £120 a day.'

The farmer explained that he was the third generation of his family on this farm and that their cows had always drunk out of the river. 'Your farm, your field, your cows, our water, you have to pay for it. Do you have any other livestock I've not seen?' 'Only a few sows in the wood, but they drink mains water' says the farmer. They go to the wood and find five sows lying at their ease in a muddy hollow. 'Your sows, your mud, but it's our water in the mud, £1 a pig a week.' Thus far the farmer has kept his temper, because you fall out with the EA at your peril, but as they walk back to the farm it starts to rain. 'This rain is water,' says the farmer, 'who owns that?' 'The rain is sent down to us by the good Lord,' says the man, 'but as soon as it lands, it's ours.'

So, belatedly, we come back to my brother's garden, and his brook and his two ponds. He's dug out two lovely ponds next to the brook, (stream, river), which keeps them replenished. So last autumn he tells me he would like some mallard ducks on the ponds. I tell him that he can easily buy mallard ducklings but until they can fly they will need protecting from predators. We go into the detail of this and it puts him off for a bit. Then one day he tells me a pair of wild mallard are visiting the ponds regularly and in order to encourage them to breed there he was thinking of buying a floating duck house. It's an interesting aside that I'm fairly sure that he didn't know that such things existed until a politician bought one on his expenses. Whatever, he bought one and secured it in the larger pond. On successive occasions he was able to report that the mallard duck had climbed into the duck house, that she had made a nest and eventually laid five eggs. The sixth egg didn't get laid because next time he looked in to see how many eggs there were all that was to be seen was feathers, blood and egg shell. There's been mink in the area before. A few years ago the mink hounds came up the stream, all blue coats and proper socks, and found a whole mink family in the bank which were dug out and dispatched.

Another time he saw a mink up a culvert, phoned a neighbour who waited for an hour for it to come back out and he shot it. My brother is suitably upset about the duck and her eggs. The mallard drake stayed three days on the pond waiting for her to reappear before he flew away. 'What shall I do now?' 'Get a trap, catch it and kill it, and then you might get some ducks again next year.' But this raises an interesting question. I'm always banging on about balance. If it were up to me, I would hunt down every last mink in the country and destroy it; it's an alien species, a relentless killer of wildlife and has no place here. I'd then take a bit of a breather and then I'd start on the grey squirrel and clear out every last one of them. In two or three generations, people might start to see red squirrels on a regular basis.

The episode with the mallard duck in my brother's garden was so upsetting for him after his vision of a brood of ducklings being reared in his garden. But what if it wasn't a mink, what if it was an otter? I honestly don't know what I'd think. I've never seen an otter in the wild and would love to do so. They went to the brink with population but now have recovered remarkably. I would have to take a more pragmatic view. There's plenty of mallard about, you can buy them, so until there's a plague of otters, well we'll just have to let them get on with what otters do.

April 30th 2011

I'm fairly sure that last year we had a dry April. This year the dry weather started in March. I thought this was better. 'We'll have the rain in April this year and grow some good crops.' Well we had a dry March and as I write to you today we've had a very dry half of April. I don't think sheep farmers have ever had lambing weather like it. I don't think there's been a day for six weeks that they haven't been able to turn newly-born lambs out every day. What I do know is that the spring corn that we rushed to get in, appeared after a shower one night, and is making no progress at all. I know that the 25 acres of winter wheat on our very top field needed some nice warm rain six weeks ago to make a decent crop of it and it is still waiting, thirsty, with its tongue hanging out. I also know that just by writing about dry weather, the weather itself will break, there will be relentless rain for weeks, floods everywhere, and it will all be down to me.

★★★

It's a nice sunny evening and there's just me and Mert going around the stock and the crops in the truck. There's something nagging at me that goes all the way back to my school days that reminds me that it should be Mert and I to be correct. I've written me and Mert quite deliberately because he's getting a bit full of himself lately, trying to dominate my life and, 'Me and Mert', puts him back in second place, but only just. Nearly all our fields have six metre boundaries around them for wildlife: 'they' call them wildlife corridors, I don't think I'm supposed to drive on them but I'm sure there are worse things going on in the world and they are very handy for driving around the outside of crops. As time passes, these six metre margins change in the composition and don't do what they were supposed to do. Apart from the corridor aspect they were also supposed to allow grasses to go to seed so that there would be food in the winter for those birds that eat seed. Slowly but surely they have been taken over by small saplings and briars, at the expense of the grasses. Some of these saplings, mostly thorn and willow, are two or three inches thick now and the grassy wildlife corridor was quickly heading towards thicket status. But now my agent tells me that the rules have changed and we can cut all this stuff back so that it's grassy again. Just like that: 'we' got it wrong, now you put it right. I sometimes think that whoever 'they' are, they make it all up as they go along. But we continue our journey around the farm and as it is evening, brown shapes can be seen in corn and grassland. At the end of my journey I've counted 23 brown hares and I'm well pleased. On Saturday morning I come across the keeper, (I'm never sure if I've come across him or he's sneaked up on me), I tell him, sort of triumphantly, about the 23 hares. 'Well you've got a lot more than that; you want to go up there at night.' So I feel a bit put down, and well pleased at the same time.

★★★

I squashed and killed a toad this morning. Well how was I to know he was in my welly?

May 2ND 2011

It's 2nd of May; outside the fields are white with frost but it's nice and cosy here in the kitchen. No worries about frost for the two dogs, who sleep comfortably on the floor by the Rayburn in the early morning. In fact the kitchen is equally comfortable for the three of us, at this pre-wife time of day. But it's not all that comfortable for me. There's a big decision afoot.

The corgi, because of her promiscuity on several previous occasions, is due at the vets today for an operation. I'm never sure if they call it spay or if that's a river in Scotland. It had been a simple decision at the time, to book her in for the operation, but now the day is here, doubts are setting in. I look at them on the floor. I'm not sure how old Mert is, and if I ask the people where he came from, they are not sure either. They try to identify it with some farming event or other like 'the year that cow got stuck in the river' or 'the year the weather spoilt a bit of hay'. But they can't really put a date on it, so Mert could be six or then he could be eight, because 'Wasn't he born that year there was a good ewe trade?' How would I know?

I do notice that he's aged a bit lately and there's more grey around his muzzle. He only tries to bite about one in ten of our visitors now; it used to be more the 50/50. Then I look at the corgi, and realise it's like having a fox in the kitchen without the smell. She's got her life in front of her, she could have corgi fox pups. We used to have a pack of three corgis that were a delight and I could just fancy that again. There are two very different operations that could be done that would resolve the issue of collie-cross-corgi pups. I could go 'eeny meeny' or I could be decisive. Decisive time, it's - pause for effect and tension - Mert. I take him at nine o'clock, because it's a bit like going to the dentist for me, get it over with quick. For Mert it's much worse, but he doesn't know that. You should never transfer human hopes and aspirations to animals. I go to collect him later. I'm not that comfortable. 'He's not very friendly, your dog,' says the nurse, so that bit hasn't changed. My big worry is that he won't speak to me, but he does and is pleased to see me. 'Keep the site clean,' says the vet. 'He can do that himself.' It's next day, the frost is on the lawn and the dogs are by the Rayburn. There's no going back now, the job is done. Mert had a habit of going off on walkabout in the spring looking for romance and I used to worry about him getting run over. Perhaps I've saved his life.

Summer

May 7th 2011

I told you about my crop of winter wheat up on my top field and how poor it looked after the hard winter. I also told you that I thought that its only hope lay in a good drink of water at the start of March. Well we all know it didn't get its drink and to be honest, I don't go to see it very often because there is nothing I can do to help it. I knew that the only decision open to me was to write it off and to start again with something else. It wasn't a decision I wanted to have to make, not before it had a good soak of rain. In the weather forecast there was always the chance of heavy showers in four days' time, but it was always in four days' time and neither rain or showers turned up.

But I do have a friend who advises me on my arable crops and he walks up there twice a week. He used to walk his spaniel up there but now he takes two spaniels because he's bought a little pup. He reckons it's one of the finer sights you will see, a ten week-old spaniel chasing a hare, the pup going flat out and the hare trotting along just that bit faster whilst looking nonchalantly over its shoulder. Anyway he comes in to the kitchen and says, 'That winter wheat has altered beyond recognition, I don't know why, but it has.' This perks me up no end, so I do have a crop after all, I don't have to write it off and start again with something else. 'It's gone from a complete disaster and will now just *almost* make a very, very poor crop.' So now I don't know how to feel.

★★★

I've got two beef calves to take to market. It's Good Friday and there is a special store cattle sale on. The place is buzzing and places to park are difficult to find. There's a huge entry of cattle plus a lot of sheep and you can almost detect the tension in the air. There are farmers there to buy cattle and as the trade for cattle is 'on fire' it's a big day for them. They have the fields, they have the grass, they always buy cattle in the spring, but they know that to pay too much will take any margin there will be, so it's a very important day out and it's important not to get it wrong. Equally tense are the people selling cattle for all the same reasons. If they have a large bunch to sell, it is important to their year's profitability, it's cost a lot to feed animals this winter because cereals have been so expensive and their dilemma has been: 'Do I sell the corn or do I feed it to my animals?'

They are about to find out the answer to that question. Held in a particular awe are the 'big men from off' (never been sure where 'off' is). These big men might not be physically very tall, but they usually have a big car, and they are 'big' because of the number of cattle that they might or might not buy. If there's enough of these men and they are looking to fill a big double decker artic with cattle, they will make a huge difference to the overall trade today.

While everyone seems to hustle and bustle about, they have an affected nonchalance. They get out of the Merc or Range Rover and put on their market day boots. They usually wear leggings to keep their trousers away from flying poo and the most essential badge of their trade is a smock. You need a smock before you even buy the cattle. As it turns out, the trade is very good. Cattle seem to be scarce, the trade in finished prime cattle is excellent and that drives the trade for these cattle that need to grow on for finishing. It's not always easy to value calves but mine make £50 apiece more than I expect. I've noticed this phenomenon in farmers before. If something is expensive, be it cattle, sheep, silage, hay, straw, whatever, they all want it and inevitably make it more expensive for themselves. If something looks really cheap, they avoid it like the plague. I've seen it so often. 'That looks cheap' says a man to his neighbour, 'No trade on them, you wouldn't want to buy them at any price.' In fact, one of the lessons I have learnt is that if you do the opposite of what all the other farmers do, there's a fair chance it will turn out OK.

May 14TH 2011

My grumbles about the continual dry weather have come to nothing, in that they haven't made it rain. Crops everywhere are now what we call stressed, especially the spring-sown crops. At a distance you can even see winter corn and grassland starting to go brown where the soil is shallower. My dry cows are short of grass and we've had to start feeding silage to a group of calves. My last throw of the dice in my attempts to influence the weather will be later this week when we cut our silage, which is always a signal for some rain. The whole situation is made worse by frosts at night and a bitter easterly wind. We have two flowering cherry trees in front of our house that come out in the last week of April (which shows how a late the season can be where we live). Their beauty was short-lived because their blossom was soon scattered to the west by the wind, like confetti, which was appropriate, given the week, but a shame. The crops may be stressed but not me. Gave up worrying about things I can do nothing about years ago.

***

We are just in the position that we need a new bull. We use a beef bull on about half our cows to breed beef cross calves to sell at 3-4 weeks old. The bull we have now is called a British Blue, a breed that used to be called Belgian Blue. Most people get quite excited about buying a 'new' bull. I'm not so content. The bull we have now is getting old and will soon struggle to do the work we expect of him (if you can call it work!). But his calves are small, easily born, lively and go on to sell well. That could all change with a different bull, but you won't know for nine months and by then there will be lots of calves in the pipeline. Caution is the order of the day.

MAY 21ST 2011

Most of our cows have made their way home for morning milking by the time my son makes his early start, so he begins by milking what's there, as the stragglers continue to wander home at their leisure. They go into the milking parlour in batches of 24 and he only usually has to get the dog around this last batch to get them in. Sometimes it's Stephen who works here who arrives at 6.30ish who gets them in; sometimes they end up doing it together. So they both get quite excited when the last 20 or 30 cows are coming up the track with the dog behind them and with two deer amongst them. The deer soon break away and are off at speed towards the woods. I didn't get excited because I didn't see them; I was here in the kitchen writing this for you. Next day I saw one of the deer in my neighbour's field. We all thought it was quite nice to see them but I don't expect they'll be about long. Too many rifles about here and a deer carcase is worth a lot of money.

★★★

A local wedding is only a couple of weeks away now and preparations are gathering momentum. The ladies, who are friends and family, pampered themselves with a night at a spa a few weeks ago but they went a bit more down to earth on Saturday when 20 of them hired a bus and went on a pub-crawl. They got back to our local at about 11, all strappy tops, pink cowboy hats and high spirits. They were a bit noisy for me, but it got better when they went into the other bar for some karaoke. But if you sit there quietly on the settle they come back one by one for a bit of male company.

They told me they'd had a really good time, thoroughly enjoyed it, the only downside was the bus driver, whose name apparently is Irritable Eric. It's never failed to surprise me what women who have been drinking will sit down and tell you quietly about other women. They tell me because they know I don't gossip! I can't write it all down here but I'll tell you when I see you. All I can say is that a woman who moved into the village twelve months ago, well she's no better than she should be. I slipped away at 1.30. Told the missus I got home at eleven and got away with it. The pub lights were still on when we went to milk next morning!

★★★

I told you we were thinking of buying a 'new' bull. It's not as easy a job as you think, especially if you have an instinct to search out a bargain. There's plenty of bulls about at plenty of money but finding a good bull that's cheap, well, that's the challenge. Then it's not straightforward either. These British Blue bulls come in different colours. Some are almost entirely black, which is OK, but they will sire calves out of dairy cows that are also black, which isn't what I want. I want calves with blue markings to sell at 3–4 weeks old. I want them to have blue markings so that there is no doubt about their breeding. What I want, I am told, is a white 'blue' bull with a pink nose.

So I see this advert and phone up. 'How much is the bull you have advertised?' 'Boy, he's a good bull, probably the best one I've ever bred, his father was one of the best bulls you'll ever see and won lots of prizes at shows.' 'Yes, but how much do you want for him?' 'He's from a proven strain of easy calving bulls and his calves are very lively and grow on quickly and well.' 'What sort of money are you looking for?' 'A bunch of his calves topped the market at 12 months old; folks said they were the best bunch of steers they'd ever seen.' The promotional spiel continues in much the same vein, unabated, and I'm inclined to let him talk on and go and make a cup of tea. I can't get a word in and I don't think he'd know if I wasn't there. But eventually he does run out of steam and while he pauses to think if there's some accolade of this particular bull he's forgotten, I'm in there. 'How much is that bull you have advertised?' '£6,000.' '£6,000! I only wanted to buy a bull; I didn't want to buy your farm as well!'

MAY 28TH 2011

When I was a little boy I kept hens in our back garden. It was, I suppose, my first steps on the farming ladder. I've climbed that ladder a lot higher since then but the higher you go, the more rubbery the ladder becomes and it is inclined to bend over with your weight and tip you off down to the bottom, where you just kept a few hens in the back garden. I was an industrious little farmer and used to breed my own replacement poultry by selecting a suitable hen and a cockerel to produce eggs that I would hatch out under a broody hen. These hens would guard their eggs with their lives, usually only coming off the nest once a day for a quick drink, some snatched food and to get rid of 24 hours worth of poo. While they completed these three tasks they would stagger about on legs that had become stiff from being in the same position since the previous day.

Thus it is with hen pheasants sitting eggs; I often wonder how they survive. When they stagger forth once a day, there's no food and water close at hand put there by a dedicated little boy. I have no idea what they find to eat, perhaps an insect or two that happens to pass by, and there's rarely water close at hand. As they sit their eggs, they become more emaciated and weaker and weaker and end up like anorexic super models that could wear a size 0 dress, whatever that might be. If their nest is on the side of a road, they usually end up under the wheels of a car. So I'm driving up a farm lane on my rounds when one of these broody hen pheasants pops out 30 yards in front of me, so I stop to give it time to sort itself out. Out of nowhere over the hedge comes a Red Kite, like a stealth bomber, and in one easy motion picks up the pheasant and takes it away. It passes quite close to me as it goes off and I can see the pheasant looking around, probably wandering what's going on. Life can be hard for a hen pheasant sitting eggs, in fact it can be a bit of a bugger.

★★★

The keeper grows maize for his pheasants; it's placed strategically so that on shooting days the pheasants that feed there fly back to their rearing pens over the guns. It's his best drive; he made the mistake of telling me that because he grows the maize on my land and has to pay me for the privilege. The money is quite handy and it means he's always nice to me. In the spring there are to be seen the tattered remnants of his maize crop and on my adjacent grass field there are to be seen the corncobs that various birds have carried there to see if an odd grain of maize is left: there must be or there wouldn't be so many cobs on my field.

I'm driving down this field last week looking about me for wildlife incidents, and I say to myself, 'Look there's a grey squirrel with a stick in its mouth.' My journey takes me close to the squirrel who has stopped at the fence that leads into the wood. I'm now sitting only five yards away from him in the truck. He's not bothered by my presence; he's more concerned with getting through the netting of the wire fence with the stick in his mouth, his 'stick' being a maize cob. It will only go through the gap if he puts one end through first and it's amazing watching him as he tries to force it through, but it won't go.

He's got one eye on me all the time and that proves to be vital to his success because he half turns his head which inadvertently puts one end of the cob through the hole. The rest of the cob and the squirrel quickly follow. As he disappears into the undergrowth he gives one last look at me over his shoulder. He's well pleased with himself.

June 4th 2011

We did over 100 acres of first cut silage this year. It's quite a large area relative to the land we farm and it's a 100 acres denuded, stripped of its crop, and it disturbs the wildlife. It lifts the lid off those fields and you can see what's about. Next day, after we've finished silage, I drive around each field, sort of assessing them. I'm really looking for hares, and there's lots of them. I don't bother to count after 20, because it could be two or three hares legging about all over the place but I'm fairly sure it isn't. Not for the first time, I drive away thinking how lucky I am.

★★★

The momentum of the local wedding gathers pace. The men, the stags, having been to Benidorm a few weeks ago, decide to have a reunion with a ten o'clock breakfast (with beer) in the pub and then they're off on a coach-driven pub crawl around our valley. To the casual observer it's interesting to watch them return to the pub, one by one, on the Saturday evening. I've always thought nonchalance was an interesting word.

All the participants were nonchalant when they came back. It's not easy to be nonchalant when you've just come through the door and ricocheted off each door post on unsteady legs. It was interesting watching them standing in the middle of the room trying to appear sensible when they are standing leaning forward at an angle approaching 45°. It was apparent to me that, should they stand leaning backwards, even 1°, they would have fallen over. A lady came into the pub later and reported having seen at least two of them fast asleep in the bottom of hedges as she walked through the village. Both in a bed of nettles.

★★★

We have a monthly 'diners' club in our village pub. It has a hard core of about 25 members. It's polarised a bit into two tables of them and us, 'locals' and newcomers, which is a shame really because if you are a newcomer, how can you become a local apart from by mixing? Last night we had wild boar sausage and mash with red onion gravy followed by rhubarb crumble and custard or ice cream or evaporated milk, in tins! As we try to stick to local dishes, it becomes harder and harder. Suggestions fly about. 'Let's have rabbit.' 'I'm not eating rabbit, not since the myxomatosis.' 'What about fat bacon and duck eggs?' Cries of disgust from the ladies. 'We used to eat badger ham and eggs when I was a boy.' (Road kill of course if you ate it today), but nobody showed any enthusiasm for badger.

★★★

Any lingering remorse I have had about having Mert 'seen to' is slipping away. It's some time since he had the snip. A friend was showing me some pictures on her computer of corgi cross permutations. Not a good idea, crossing your corgi. The most attractive, and that was relative, was a corgi cross poodle. Which is interesting because a poodle cross Labrador is a very popular cross. Always fancied a poodle, not a tarted up trimmed one, but an around the yard sort of poodle.

Dog crosses are interesting. Years ago, when I was doing a fair bit of shooting, someone gave me two Labrador cross spaniels. I was really excited about training them to work. A friend told me that all I would get would be the worst traits of both breeds in one dog. He was right. When you loosed them for a run around, you only had to turn your back for a second and they would both be in the next parish, but not the same parish. The best cross dog we ever had (we've had a lot of dogs) was a spaniel crossed with a Jack Russell terrier. He was called Freddie and he looked like a small version of a Bassett hound. He was a bit of a free spirit.

There's a weekend cottage three fields away down our lane, the family used to come most weekends and kept a basket and food for Freddie and he would go down the lane every day to see if they were there. If they were, he would stay until they went home again. At school holiday times we wouldn't see him for days, weeks, on end. Anyway I'm down the vets one day and while I'm waiting in the queue, I'm reading the adverts they have on their board, and I come across a note about a dog being found and a description of the dog. 'That sounds just like our Freddie.' Then I realise I haven't seen him for some time, but that was not unusual. So I get the receptionist to phone the number. Turns out it's the site of a local permanent traveller's camp. (Permanent and travellers seems to me a contradiction, but I'll tread carefully on).

So I drive across there and there's Freddie helping them sort out some scrap metal. So it's all very friendly and I tell them he's our dog, they see that anyway, because he's already sitting on the front seat of my truck. I take him home and he is obviously pleased to be reunited with his family and he spends a happy day with us. When we say goodnight to him he's on his blanket by the Rayburn. He manages to get the kitchen door open during the night and so when I get up to milk next morning he's stretched out comfortably on the settee. He comes to fetch the cows with me, not that he's interested in cows, he just thinks I'm taking him for a walk.

When I finish milking, he's nowhere to be seen but on a hunch I drive to the traveller's camp. It's six miles from here but there he is, having his breakfast in a caravan. The family beg me to let him stay, 'We go to the seaside in the summer; he'll love that.' That was the last I saw of him. At the time I was preoccupied with the thought that dairy farming had reached a really low ebb if your dog preferred to go off and live with travelling folk. But there was more to it than that. How did Freddie know that dairy farming would get even worse? Should have taken more notice of Freddie. It's amazing what animals know.

June 11ᵀᴴ 2011

One of the rewards of farming is the pleasure that comes from the ownership of livestock. Next to that comes having good crops in your fields, be it, in my case, cereals or grass. And I like my fields to look tidy. If a Welshman looks over your hedge and says, 'There's tidy,' that will do nicely for me. Nettles, docks and thistles do their very best to undermine 'tidy' and to be fair to them, they are remorseless in their efforts and as they contribute nothing of any value to the farm, you have to be remorseless in your efforts to control them. 'People' are starting to express concerns about the long-term supply of food on this planet. Oxfam were talking about it recently. It's trendy to blame global warming, but I am sceptical about that (I still carry the mental scars of the cold last winter). I think it's more to do with too many mouths to feed in 20 years' time and the wasteful way we treat food.

If someone could find a way of making nettles, thistles and docks palatable, all our troubles would disappear. Nettles in particular, if left unchecked, would quickly take over the world; it wouldn't be much of a world mind, you'd get your legs stung all day long. I went down to my daughter's farm one day. I met her and her two children doing a bit of bike riding on their lane. My daughter and granddaughter were wearing shorts and strappy tops. My grandson was wearing a balaclava, a long coat, gloves, long trousers, and wellies. It was a lovely sunny day, 'Why has that boy got all that tack on?' 'He's frightened he'll fall off his bike into the nettles.'

★★★

Most years on the farm I try to identify something we can do better. This year is the year of the nettle. Nettles have been winning the battle for too many years and this year they were to get their come-uppance. In the past we would attack the nettles with a sprayer on our back, doing a spot treatment of nettles.

Everybody hated the job. It was hard, uncomfortable work. When full, the sprayer weighed over 50lbs, and the little breather hole in the lid would allow spray to slurp down your neck. You could wear a waterproof coat with the collar turned up but on a hot day, a good nettle-spraying day, that made the job even more uncomfortable. It used to amuse me, that the label on the spray would say: avoid contact with your skin. It would start off running down your neck, down your back, down the backs of your legs and eventually wet your socks. It's never done me any harm; I think I'd have had my nervous twitch anyway.

Left to their own devices, people don't do jobs they don't like, so last year I bought an electric sprayer that sits in the back of the Discovery and we drive around the field with a hand lance out of the window, spraying clumps of nettles as we go. But even that didn't get many outings last year: hence my determination this year. We've bought a new second-hand topper to cut the thistles regularly and I've been busy at it every time I've had time and the weather has allowed. I'm inclined to use the phrase 'warming to my task' and I have been. So yesterday, after tea and quite a long day, I'm off on the tractor to tidy up some thistles with the topper rather than take it easy. As the evening progressed, the hares started to come out of the woods; most clumps of thistles contained a poor-looking cock pheasant, mostly limping after numerous battles. I 'topped' until nine o'clock and when I left to go home I looked back over the gate and thought to myself, 'There's tidy indeed.'

June 18th 2011

When is a farmer not a farmer? There's probably lots of answers to that question but one of them is, when he's in his 80s and has no younger person, employee or relative, to help him on his farm. I know of a few cases like that. They are usually remarkably determined old men who still keep a few cattle or sheep but when something tricky turns up, they rely on friends or neighbours to help them out. 'Just' is an important word in their vocabulary. 'You couldn't just come down and give me a hand to calve this cow?' 'You wouldn't just come down and help me catch this ewe?' We were talking about just such a case the other day: a man left on his own and farming about 60 acres and keeping about 12 beef suckler cows and their progeny. The cows and their calves have the run of the farm in the winter and can come in to the buildings when and how they want. He would put big bales of silage out for them every day with his ancient tractor and loader and every day if he had any sense he would bolt back in to his warm kitchen during the worst days of last winter, so the cattle wouldn't have had much human contact and they happen to be Charolais cows, which are huge. So this story starts as I first described, a phone call to a friend of mine: 'You couldn't just pop down, I'm having trouble calving a heifer.' Which proved to be an understatement.

★★★

It's a strange phenomenon cattle behaviour. Dairy cows out in a field are usually quiet. Dairy bulls are always aggressive and dangerous and are rarely seen out in fields unless they are very young and even then should be away from a footpath. Beef bulls are usually very quiet and rarely pose any threat to anyone. Beef cows are usually very quiet unless they have calves with them, when they can be very dangerous, especially if strange dogs are about. I've used the 'usually' quite deliberately here, because cattle should never be taken for granted. Cattle of all sorts may chase a strange dog but beef cows will chase it to attack it and that's why we occasionally hear of tragedies occurring and if ever you find yourself in that sort of situation, it's best to let the dog go, because most dogs are fleet enough of foot to take care of themselves. So my friend goes down and there's this huge Charolais heifer in the early stages of calving and she's gone berserk. Not as in sort of mentally ill, but as in aggressively attacking anything that moves.

My friend and the old man have a look over the gates at her and she charges across the shed and hits the gate so hard that the whole building rattles including the roof sheets. They retreat to the safety of a stack of bales and climb up and watch her. She's watching them and she stands there tossing her head and making small charges in their direction. 'I've phoned the vet to come and help,' says the old man.

A lady vet turns up after a while; she's our vet too and well up for anything. So the three of them make a plan. They will put one of those huge bales of straw on the loader and use it to push the heifer into a corner where they can hold her against the wall while the vet attends to the calving. And it works, for a while: the heifer is pressed against the wall by the straw bales and the old man stays on the tractor and the other two go to assist the calving.

But not for long. With a mighty roar she lifts the bale and the loader and escapes and turns to attack. The only escape for the two on the floor is to dive into the tractor cab with the old man. It's an old tractor with a small cab and it's a bit of a squeeze for three but it's the only safe place to go. They could, if they wished, drive the tractor about the shed, but on no account can they get out because the heifer is repeatedly charging the tractor with such force that the rear wheels come off the floor. This was a hilarious story in the pub but in reality it was life and death stuff. One of them says to the vet, 'Pity you can't sedate her.' The vet says, 'If I can get close enough to put a needle in her, she'll never get up again.' Which, also in reality, is what should happen to an animal like this because one day it could kill someone, especially someone in their 80s who is not the quickest on their feet.

So the story comes to a close. All this charging about and attacking things has another effect, and there in the straw is a new-born calf, none the worse for the activities of its mother. This is the sort of distraction our heroes and heroine need, and the tractor is driven close to the gate and they squeeze out of the cab and over the gate and to safety. Not that they feel that safe: even with a gate between them and a ton of heifer. They beat a hasty retreat. As I said, beef cows are usually quiet, unless there are calves with them.

June 25th 2011

I knew a man who farmed and lived in a sort of twilight world. I don't think that the Inland Revenue or the National Insurance people knew he existed, in fact, very few people who wanted money off him knew he was there, yet strangely, if the money was to come in the other direction, for example sheep subsidy, he knew all about that and made sure he had every penny due to him. But these days, computers talk to each other and eventually officialdom found its way to his door.

They sent a young wimpish sort of man, which was their first mistake because my man was over six feet tall and over 20 stone, rarely shaved and was altogether a fearsome sight. Suffice to say that the young man spent an hour in the kitchen penned into a corner by four nasty sheep dogs, failed to deliver any message or receive any on-going commitment until he was allowed to flee, not back to the office but straight home where he stayed for a whole week. But the system is made of sterner stuff and undeterred they tried again.

Next time they sent a more senior man, chosen not only for his seniority, but he was big with it. He dressed himself in a tweedy sort of outfit and some of those wellies with buckles on like they wear on *Spring Watch* and *Lambing Live*. So our big civil servant man turns up in the yard in his smart rural outfit and is immediately surrounded by a ring of snarling dogs. Ring is an appropriate configuration because our man comes around the corner, walks around him a couple of times, comments on and admires his attire and suggests that before they get down to business, they try a few wrestling throws. Undeterred the man starts to deliver his message but it's not done with much dignity because by now he's held in a bear hug and his feet are two feet off the ground. To his relief he is not thrown to the ground but put back down gently and invited into the kitchen. He sees this as a good sign and thinks a spell of small talk will help ease the situation.

My farmer always wore wellies, He wore them in hot weather in the summer and it was rumoured he wore them in bed in the winter. So he notes the fine pair of wellies his visitor is wearing and says that he has never seen such a fine pair of wellies and can he have a look at one of them. One thing leads to another and he has to walk about a bit in them in the kitchen. But that's not the same as outside and so he has to try them out on the yard, and if the official is to keep in touch he has no alternative but to put on the two discarded wellies and follow him outside. The visit swiftly comes to an end: the farmer gets into the tractor and disappears down a narrow track in a veritable cloud of mud and dogs. The visitor returns to his 'suited' office in his rural outfit wearing a pair of nondescript wellies that have always been worn half turned down and with a bicycle inner tube repair patch on one toe.

July 2ND 2011

Trendy people, and you will know that I'm not one of them, say trendy things. Things like 'Blue sky thinking' and 'I dipped into a programme on TV.' I dipped into the recent *Springwatch* programme and seemed to coincide my 'dips' with the debate on the ravages of predator birds on songbirds including actual pictures of this activity going on. The activities of magpies came under particular scrutiny. The man from the RSPB said that there was no evidence anywhere that magpies affected populations of songbirds. He would say that wouldn't he, because he, like most of his colleagues, have their heads in the sand on this issue. What he didn't say, which was quite a surprise, is that the songbird decline is all down to farmers which is always the easy shot and which 'they' always use when they are cornered in an argument.

I recently came across a discussion on the decline of turtle-doves, all down to farmers removing their habitat. There was just one paragraph at the end to say that these birds, on their journeys, run the gauntlet of most of the shotguns in Europe, which apparently has little effect at all.

Driving my tractor gives me the privilege of a mobile hide from which to watch wildlife. I find it quite distressing to watch a family of magpies walking about on the top of a hedge. From their activity and from the way they disappear into the hedge, you know that there is a family of songbirds newly fledged within that hedge, and it is not until the magpies fly away do you know that they have all been despatched. It distresses me but you should see the distress of the poor parents. So if you agree that songbird numbers are down, why let the corvidae eat more of them? If magpies were to become rare, you would soon find me well on their side but they are not and there is an issue of balance that needs addressing.

★★★

Since my mother passed away I've never been sure if anyone reads what I write. She used to read everything I wrote and with that knowledge came the confidence that it was a worthwhile experience, if only for her benefit. So what I am going to say next is the sort of thing that I would unburden myself with to my mother. In the last 12 months, both my wife and I have had 'big' birthdays. Hers was before mine, which makes me a sort of toyboy. Her party was a surprise.

On reflection, surprise parties are excellent. In order to keep the secret there is no preparation required in the way of tidying the place up. There were three things she didn't want: she didn't want a party, she didn't want another corgi and she didn't want the birthday anyway. She couldn't do anything about the latter but a party and a corgi she did have.

My party was planned. So we had to tidy up, especially in the garden. Luckily our garden has views that are spectacular. So you don't have to tidy that much because everyone is looking at the view. I thought, if I get the lawns looking nice, that will do. We borrowed an outside bar from the pub, and a tent to go with it, and hired a small marquee and had a pig roast.

Getting the lawns looking nice has not been easy this year. There have been moles in it everywhere. I try to catch them and when I mow the lawns I just drive through the molehills and spread them about. But the corgi sees herself as a top mole catcher and as a result we don't just have a bare patch of soil where the moles have come up, we have a hole to go with it where she's been digging. She justifies this action with the dead mole she carries triumphantly about. I think she stole it off a cat.

A week before the party and half the lawn is standing in water, there's a burst somewhere. I phone the plumbers and they turn up when I'm not about. So they have a mini digger in there looking for a burst pipe. I happen to know that there are no water pipes anywhere near the lawn and the water will have 'travelled' from somewhere else and popped up in the lawn. By now some of the lawn is waterlogged, some of it has been dug up but that's quite handy because, it takes three barrowfuls of soil to fill up the holes the corgi has dug. And the views are still nice.

The party was OK as well. On the invites I said I didn't want presents, but I didn't really mean it. I suggested a donation to the NSPCC and we are over £600 now. I suppose we could have had the party in the house but there were a few people there I wouldn't want in our house anyway.

JULY 11TH 2011

If you happen to go into the pub in the early evening at weekends, occasionally there are people in there that have been drinking all day. Mostly its best keep a bit of a distance because they are in a place that you are unlikely to reach that evening, and even if you did, they would have staggered home by then and left you on your own. What they have to say is much funnier, more profound and wiser than anything they have ever heard themselves say ever before but to you, the sober spectator, it is much less so. There's a young attractive girl dominating the conversation, I think she's 50 this year, but sitting where I am, at my stage in life, she's young and attractive.

She's telling her immediate audience about something and I'm not paying that close attention, but then, to prove her point, she says 'Well you wouldn't eat yellow snow would you?' Now there's a profound thought for you. Must say I'd never thought about that before. But you wouldn't, would you? You'd ask yourself, instinctively, how did it get yellow? Then you'd work out how it got yellow, you'd realise the most obvious solution and you just wouldn't eat yellow snow! I'm just thinking about this yellow snow and thinking that the subtlety of what she's said is lost on her friends but not a bit of it.

Someone else takes up the theme. 'My old granny used to rush to get to town on market day. She liked to get to the grocers as soon as they opened the doors. We had to have a pony and trap ready for her first thing and away she'd go, whipping away at that old pony and he'd be a picking his feet up just as fast as he could go.'

The small group pause to replenish their glasses and I worry that I'll not hear any more about granny going shopping on market day, but not a bit of it, the story continues without any bits of it seeming to go missing. 'The one big grocers in town used to stock a big pile of round cheeses on their doorstep, a column either side, great big cheeses they were, 30lbs in weight, as a sort of display. Every damn dog that came down that street used to cock his leg against the pile of cheeses and granny was making sure that her cheese came off the top of the pile. If ever we had some poor cheese Granddad would say 'I can taste border collie on this cheese, Mother.'

Someone from a generation or so less takes up the theme. 'When we were kids we were told never to pick blackberries below waist height down by the lakes.' Someone asks why not. 'Because of the fishermen.' And that's it. Good practical advice that I can store and remember, and no one has used the word P.

★★★

I never wish to sound pretentious, but over the years, we as a family, have bought a lot of cars and vehicles off the same person. There we are, that's pretentious but taking into account all our extended family and that we mostly buy five or six year old cars and keep them three or four years. Multiply that by 30 years, that's quite a lot of cars. It all started well over 30 years ago when a vehicle I had bought was really crap and the main dealer gave me my money back. As a result I'm in the position for the first time to play the field with no part exchange. So I'm looking in the small ads for a run-of-the-mill family car and I see this three-year-old Saab at an unbelievably low price for a Saab and I meet this man on a lay-by and we do a deal.

Four years later we think of changing again and so we dig out his phone number and the rest is history. But although he has become a friend he would not be upset if I said that he operates at the lower end of the car market, no showroom, just a one-man-band who underwrites deals at other garages, so he sometimes offers you a car and you get a bit excited about it and the car never turns up, but not to worry because there's soon another car to get excited about. What he is good at, very good at, is the diagnosis of problems. He lives an hour and a half away so if I have a problem I phone him and so far he's always been right.

So we come to the job in hand: my son has a five-year-old 4x4 that won't go into four-wheel-drive. For years you engaged four-wheel-drive vehicles with a lever and it worked well but 'progress' dictates that four-wheel-drive is engaged by sensors and these go wrong and there's five of them and you can't tell which sensor isn't working so you have to buy five and they're expensive, so you phone your man.

We arrange to meet half way and he'll bring me a car to get home in. 'You can have a Mondeo, a Corsa or a Camper van.' 'Are any of them taxed and insured?' 'Only the Camper van.' 'I'll have the Camper.' It's an old Camper and it looks like an old shed, smells a bit like an old shed as well. I didn't realise there was so much fun to be had with a Camper. In the house: 'What's that doing on the yard?' 'I've bought it.' 'Whatever for?' 'Thought we could go on holiday in it.' 'If you think I'm going on holiday with you in that thing after slaving away all year doing bed and breakfast you're mistaken, take it back.' 'Can't, I've bought it now, and besides, it will come in handy all year round.' 'What for?' 'Well they are very busy with the breathalyser round here at the moment so I can go to the pub in it, sleep in the car park and come home next morning.' Answer, unprintable.

In the pub: 'Whose is that Camper in the car park?' 'Mine, just bought it.' 'What for?' So I tell them the breathalyser story and also that the pub is always full with B&B and I'm going to do B&B in the car park with the overflow, so they all go back out to have a closer look at it and when they come back, 'Smells a bit inside.'

My son fetches his youngest son from school: 'What have you got this for?' 'We're going to Glastonbury in it.' 'When?' 'Now.' He fetches his oldest son from football (17 now). 'What's that for?' 'It's for you when you pass your test.' His face is a picture of abject misery; apparently a Camper van is not cool. If I was 17 and knew what I know now, it would be beyond my wildest dreams. But all good things come to an end. The Camper has to go back, in a hurry; someone is coming to buy it. I get a nice little Citroen to replace it. 'This goes well, how do you value something like this.' '£995, it would just suit your missus.'

JULY 23ᴿᴰ 2011

It's the time of year when I follow the cows around their grazing area with the topper. They have an area of fresh grass every day and I go into yesterday's patch and trim off all the grass that's not been eaten around the dung pats and at the same time decapitate any docks and thistles before they go to seed. There's a bit of judgement involved. We farm in a relatively low rainfall area and if I top too often there will be no grass the next time the cows rotate around their grazing area. This patchy weather is just the job because I know that I can top and the soaking of rain we've just had will ensure a good bite of grass again in three-four weeks' time.

Any tractor activity in the fields usually attracts the attention of birds and yesterday, as I'm topping a field under the wood, I'm thinking to myself that the birds are quiet today, when a buzzard drops down onto a clump of grass I've cut off. It's there for a few seconds on the ground, wings outstretched as it tussles with whatever it has found. Then it takes off with its prey. I can't see what it's got because I haven't got my glasses on, (I can never find them in the kitchen so why would I want to lose them on a tractor?) Whatever it is, it's quite large because the buzzard is obviously struggling to clear the hedge, bit like a Chinook helicopter that's picked up the biggest tank by mistake. It slowly gains height and it's off up the dingle and into the wood, where I know there is a nest.

Next day and on the next patch and I have a family of carrion crows for company. The three young ones are not flying that well yet and I wish I had my gun with me. But I never have. I dislike crows as a species because I see what they do to other birds. Every year I mean to go around and reduce their numbers but never get to it. There are a lot of magpies about as well and I've also let that chance slip away. Meanwhile the carrion crows strut about importantly in the field as they search for food. I always think that there's something of the Fat Controller about them. But suddenly they turn from self-important railway officials into World War I fighter planes. A buzzard appears in the field and I am treated to a display of aerobatics as all five crows go on the attack with a series of near misses that eventually drive the buzzard off. I'm not a big fan of buzzards either but I sympathise with the hassle they get from crows and magpies. They never seem that concerned but it must drive them to distraction.

★★★

There used to be a man had a small farm in our village, kept a few horses, kept a few cattle, kept a few hens and also a few pigs. When I look back on it now, I wonder that he made a living but he was the most contented of men, always had time for a chat, always time to go to the pub. It was his wife, who had clearly been a very beautiful woman in her time, who looked harassed and did most of the work, and I suspect it was she who had to make the ends meet.

He had, for his transportation, three big old Humber cars. They were all the same model and colour and strangely all had the same number plate. This, he explained, was very convenient because out of the three cars, there was usually one of them running and so he could put the current tax disc in whichever he was using. Everyone in the village thought that this was an eminently sensible arrangement, even the village policeman.

For breeding purposes he used to take his sows to a farm in the next village where they kept a boar. He didn't actually take them himself except for the first time. Usually after she'd been once, sows would come into season and he would just put them out on the road and they would make their way quite briskly on their own the couple of miles to where the boar lived. He would fetch them back in the little trailer behind the car.

One day the trailer had a puncture so he just took the car that was running that day and when he got there he simply opened the back door and the pig obligingly got in and stood in the space between the seats. When he got home he just had to open the other door and the pig marched out. If there were two sows at the boar, one would have to stand on the back seat. It's quite a big job, backing up to a small trailer and hitching it on, so from then on that was how he transported his sows back from the boar.

The only downside was if hens had laid on the back seat and the sows ate the eggs. I often used to meet him on the road and we would have a chat, the sow would nuzzle at the window so he would lean back and open it. 'Look at the mess she's made of the glass.' And the sow would put her head out of the window and share the conversation. If another car occasionally came along we would have to move to let them by and he would always say, 'The traffic around here is worse than Swansea.' It used to be a local saying that the traffic was worse than Piccadilly; I'd seen Piccadilly on the television but never seen or been to Swansea. I used to drive on down the lane on the tractor and think to myself, 'Must be some place, Swansea.'

JULY 30TH 2011

It's not a big deal for me but about four or five times a year I wash my car. For most of the year it is, unmistakably, a farmer's car. Well, it would be: it goes on muddy yards most days of its life. And on occasions, those occasions being the times when the car is filthy and our pressure washer is broken, I take it down to our local town and submit it to the car-washing skills of my friends from Eastern Europe. I call them friends but there's mostly a different team there every time I go. Still, they all call me boss so they must be my friends, mustn't they?

But one day I'm down there in the old 4x4 we use around the farm and I decide to throw a fiver at the outside and knock the worst of it off. So I pull into the washing bay and there are no friendly smiles, 'No, boss, the drain she block up.' This rankles a bit, any rejection in life can be hurtful whatever form it comes in, so I drive round the corner to a garage and decide I'll not be beaten and I'll wash the truck under the conventional car wash rollers. I park at the entrance to the wash and go and buy a token in the shop. I'm just getting back in when a stern voice stops me: 'Oi, just where do you think you're going with that?' I drive home disappointed. To be pragmatic, most of the mud will fall off in the dry weather.

★★★

I once knew a man who lived up in the hills near Abergavenny. Bit of a character, who had lived a varied and interesting life. When I knew him he had retired to a small farm but he had, in his time, been a chauffeur, and gardener at the 'big house'. It was at a time when the 'big house' would be the only place where you would find a car and so his ability to drive the family Rolls put him into the same sort of prestige bracket that we put astronauts.

One of his great delights was to produce wine and he was very good at it. He made his wine from almost everything you could think of. It was delightful wine and renowned locally for its potency. This was much to the consternation of his long-suffering wife who was strict Chapel and completely against all drink. He used to tell me his stories when he was an old man sitting in a comfortable chair in his immaculate kitchen garden and his wife would bustle by and scold him, 'Don't you fill that young boy's head with your old tales.' But this young boy used to love listening to him and I can still picture the scene now.

He used to fix a tall pole in each corner of his kitchen garden and put thin wires across the diagonals. Then he would have a piece of wood he had cut from a hedge; there would be the main piece about two feet long and two small branches that came off it, symmetrically. He would fix a goose wing to each of these spars and suspend the whole piece from the diagonal wires. And there it would hang like some evil bird of prey. The slightest breath of wind would float it about the garden. Birds or rabbits never came near.

He would tell me about haymaking. He would wait until all his neighbours had finished and then he would cut his. It wouldn't be a big acreage but it would be horse mower stuff. And like locusts, men would come in the evenings to turn his hay by hand, from miles around. It's always been a sort of tradition for farm workers to go and help people harvest on other farms, once the harvest was over where they worked full-time. The difference here would be that not only the workers would come, but the farmers would come as well, and it wouldn't be for a bit of extra money they came, it was for the drink.

So my man on his small farm would survey his staff of up to 20 men working away at his hay crop and he would stroll around and encourage them and dispense small quantities of wine to keep it all going smoothly, to oil the wheels as it were, and as the evening went on there would be a party atmosphere developing, good humour and shouts of encouragement would be everywhere. After they'd finished they would squeeze into his kitchen for bread and cheese and pickled onions and whatever salad was ready in his garden and eventually stagger home or go along home on their bikes and say what a good time they'd had.

The actual carting of the hay was the highlight of it all. There would be three or four horses and wagons involved and they would split into teams, each team would be tasked with clearing one of the small fields and as the drink flowed the whole operation would become competitive as they raced to clear their fields. All the hay was gathered loose and the horses would sometimes be galloped as they raced back to the yard with their load. More than one load would fall off, to great cheers from the assembled company, but all would join in good-naturedly to put the load back on.

And when all was finished and they had all gone home, my old friend would look at his full bays and reflect on the fact that he hadn't actually broken sweat in this haymaking exercise and turn his thoughts to making some more wine.

August 6th 2011

Our largest field is 40 acres; it's up on the top of our land. Because it is so big (for us) we farm it in two halves. This year, half is in grass for silage and the other half is left as stubble from last year as a haven and food-source for birds. We didn't cut the grass on this piece when we did our second cut silage, two or three weeks ago, but left it to bulk up and today I'm mowing it and tomorrow it will go into big round bales wrapped with plastic.

I'm thinking about next year, we've always got stock around the yard in the summer, mostly dry cows due to calve, and it's always handy to have a few bales of silage about. As I turn with the mower on the headland I run my eye over the part of the field that is, or was, stubble. By now it's waist high in weeds, particularly boar thistles, and it's a sight that jars on a tidy farmer's eye. Within a couple of weeks we will have combined some wheat and created a new stubble and I can get into this unsightly jungle and chop it up. As I mow further and further into the grass, an occasional hare breaks cover and lopes off at a leisurely pace into the next field. It's a fairly tranquil scene: man, tractor, mower, the sun, the sky and the view. Then we have some drama. Two leverets break cover, they are quite young and they try to run away keeping as close to the ground as possible. A hare's defences are first crouching down for concealment, and then speed. These two are trying a combination of both, but not very successfully.

So I'm driving down the field and on the other side of the last swathe I created are the two leverets, when out of nowhere appear two buzzards. The buzzards are in some dilemma: they can easily catch the leverets, speed and size are on their side, but I'm just that bit too close with my tractor and they dwell on it a bit too long. The leverets make it into the stubble jungle and safety. For a large bird it's an impenetrable mess and although they hang about for half an hour, I watch them carefully and don't see them take off with any prey. I continue with my mowing. Perhaps all those weeds and thistles aren't so bad after all.

★★★

There was another wedding in the village recently, held at the pub. Filled the car park with a marquee, most of the wedding was planned in the pub, all the lady regulars quite excited. And that excitement builds as they have the stag night, which I managed to avoid, and then the hen night, when I contrived to be in the pub when they got back: surprising what you can find out from participants at a hen night. Then a week before the big day, they ask me to be MC at the wedding, which is a bit of a surprise and gets the nerves going because I don't think I'm very good at that sort of thing.

Anyway, to get to the purpose of this anecdote, I end up in my best M&S suit with a towel round my waist held there with cling film, doing three hours in the pub kitchen, washing up. No marigolds mind: my delicate hands repeatedly pushed into hot soapy water. One of the lady guests comes into the kitchen, (very attractive too) and asks for a cup of hot water. So I give her the cup of hot water thinking she has some baby food to warm up or perhaps she drinks her own herbal tea bag instead of the coffee. Half an hour later she wants another cup of hot water. By the fifth time I tell her she is making serious inroads into my washing up water so she explains that hot water is all she ever drinks! Now there's a thing.

When I was single I only ever met girls who drank gin and tonic (married one of them), whereas all my friends met girls who drank half a mild. So here's me, been spending a fortune on alcohol for 50-odd years and all the while there are women out there who only drink hot water! No one ever told me that. Just think of the saving!

As an aside, there's a big impact on local social life around here: we have a new local policeman who keeps himself very busy at night. There are now ten locals without driving licences. So I only have two drinks now and the rest of the time I put my life at risk of ginger beer poisoning. I should be OK but you feel a bit twitchy as you drive past his parked car at 1 o'clock in the morning.

AUGUST 20ᵀᴴ 2011

I'm not one to complain about the weather, as you know, but it does have its ironies. We've had a very dry July here following a dry spring and in the last two weeks the grass we have here has just 'melted away'. It's what we call burning; it doesn't grow, it turns brown. The cows are now on just about ¾ winter rations, sheep have had to be taken off some of the local hills because they have just turned brown as well. We have one field that has a 30-yard strip across it where the soil is very thin over the rock and that strip always burns off, but this year, even the hedgerows in line with that strip have started to wilt. So when we finally do get a welcome thundery shower, where am I? Down the fields moving the electric fence without a coat and soaked to the skin. The rain is needed on the land, not on me.

★★★

As I sit in my armchair I can see out into the field in front of our house. The windowsill is only a foot high, an irresistible magnet for young children who love to swing on the curtains, the curtains have been swung on so often that if someone slams the door, they fall down. The first thing I can see in the field is a pond. Some people have called it a lake but it's a pond. It's all to do with perception. The Environment Agency did a map of our poultry unit once and highlighted a puddle and called it a lake, (the Environment Agency being big on water).

Behind our pond are some trees and for the last four springs I have happened to be in my armchair in the evening and watched an increasing number of magpies attacking the young pigeons that are about to fledge. I reckon there are about four pairs of pigeons that nest there and I find it an upsetting spectacle as wave after wave of attacking magpies go in after the unfortunate fledglings and the pigeons' parents try frantically to protect them.

Enough is enough and I borrowed a Larsen trap. In six days we have caught 11 magpies, two buzzards and two cats. The magpies have been euthanised and the cats and buzzards returned to the wild. An interesting discussion in the pub: which is the hardest to extricate from a Larsen trap, a buzzard or a wild cat.

★★★

There's the story about a farmer who lives some distance from here. He's very wide, as in nearly 30 stone wide. I think wide is a kinder word than obese, which I think is often offensive. This 'wide' man loves to do the combining but he's too wide to climb the ladder to get in the cab. So they have to put him on a pallet and lift him up to the door with a forklift. Which is OK up to a point but if he can't get up then he can't get down, and there he has to stay until they come to rescue him.

The man who drives the forage harvester for the contractors who do our silage was run over walking home from the pub one night, which wasn't very funny at the time. His legs were damaged and he finds it hard work climbing the ladder to get into the cab and that isn't funny either. But we can't do anything about it and life goes on, so I frequently make a fuss of getting a tape measure out and measuring the steps so that I can buy him a stair lift. And he gets his own back with interest.

★★★

When I was a youth working on a farm we had a boss who could be very sharp with his tongue. I once asked him for a Saturday off in hay harvest to go to a wedding. 'Course you can go, what bit of work you do won't be missed.' If he wound himself up he could get quite nasty and he would wind himself up quite often. The problem was that he had to go off every morning early to do his milk round and wouldn't be back home until lunchtime and if we were on a big job he would fret all morning about how we were getting on.

But nothing fretted him more than haymaking. It was all small bales and hard work in those days and no matter what we did, it was usually wrong, he having the benefit of hindsight on all we did. But we did have a ploy. The boss had been in an accident when he was young and orthopaedics weren't what they are now and he couldn't bend one of his legs at the knee. So we would stack the hay up as high as we could get it around the outside of the field, then bale that swathe last so as his milk truck pulled up at the gateway when he got back from his milk round.

He would be ranting and raving in the gateway and waving his arms about but he couldn't come any closer because he couldn't get his stiff legs over the swathe. Most people bale hay from the outside in, but we used to work from the middle out. We knew exactly what we were doing, he knew exactly what we were doing, the language and abuse we received was terrible, but at least it was at a distance.

Autumn

I've spent a lot of time on a tractor lately. We've been busy harvesting various crops and ploughing and reseeding grass fields and putting in turnips for winter feed. It has not escaped my notice that our No. 1 tractor has air conditioning and suspension and that I never get to drive it. 'My' tractor has no air conditioning, no suspension and the air cushion under the seat doesn't work so my spine is travelling on metal. It's quite strange putting in 10-12 hours on a tractor when your only companions are your thoughts and what's on the radio. You live in two worlds, the world that is you and machine in a field – and the outside world and its goings on, brought to you by radio.

So what's in my immediate world? Dust. We've worked up a stubble after spring wheat and I am now power-harrowing it. I'm using a machine with lots of rotating tines and the dust I am creating is the worst I've ever seen. As I write we are still in the grips of a drought. Streams dry, pastures brown and bare. Earlier this week we did 60 acres of third cut silage. It was cut on the Saturday and the plan was for the contractor to pick it up first thing Monday morning. So that's OK, but the forecast is for heavy rain on the Tuesday. The contractor still hasn't turned up by midday, the grass is beautifully wilted and I'm starting to get twitchy. So I'm on the phone to the contractor, 'We'll be there by 3, don't worry.' I had to speak at someone's birthday party last Sunday, they phoned up to thank me, 'You've got a way with words,' they said. They want to try listening to an agricultural contractor for five minutes! Eventually they turn up at 6.30pm. They break down for three hours at 9pm and we finish at 3am. I thank the team profusely for staying late before the rain came. Three days later and we've still not had a single drop!

★★★

Back on the power harrow and there's a light breeze, one way down the field and the breeze moves the dust away from me, back up the field and we are travelling at the same speed and I'm in a dust cloud all the way. Another thing about this tractor, the doors don't shut tight, so there's as much dust on me as on the tractor. In the end I have to stop quite frequently to let the dust clear because I can't see where I'm driving. The travel news comes on Radio 2. As usual it works slowly down the country, north to south. As usual there are the regular culprits. Lots of slow traffic around Manchester, hold-ups on the M6 all over the place, then the M25, I sometimes think it would be quicker to say where the M25 is clear. Today it would be much quicker!

But what's this? Flash floods in Dorset, water up to car bonnets! My tractor could do with a wash like that. For a small island, what a diversity of weather we have. Why can't we have some of that rain? They've obviously got too much. On my dust-free travel down the field I can see a few pheasants, a buzzard and some rooks, presumably looking for any grubs I have disturbed. Then out of nowhere, eight herring gulls. That's really unusual, we are at least 65 miles from the sea, why aren't they terrorising holiday-makers at the seaside and snatching chips and ice creams? Next time down the field and eight has become 22. An hour later and there are over 100. And I wonder what brought them there, where they came from, and how the last ones knew where the first eight were feeding? And I forget about the heat and the dust and I nearly forget about the crap tractor.

SEPTEMBER 10TH 2011

We have to leave 20 acres of stubble every year for the birds. You know my feeling about balance and ground-nesting birds and predators. If I thought it worked I wouldn't mind, but there we go. You leave this nice clean stubble over winter and you can't do anything with it until next harvest when you replace it with a stubble in another field. But come spring, it doesn't stay a stubble for long, weed grasses germinate and grow and boar thistles appear. You've never seen thistles like it, wall-to-wall thistles: most years they are up to the tractor bonnet, this year being very dry, up to the front wheels. You've never seen, from a farmer's point of view, a mess like it. But now we've harvested the next stubble, and we can cut it all off. I'd like to put a match to it but it's so dry I might set fire to the whole parish. It's a slow job and thistledown takes to the wind like snow.

There's only about five acres left and I go to finish it off. It's alive with hares and as I cut it down and the area left gets smaller and smaller, the more hares I see. Mostly they are half-grown leverets but my concern is the ten or twelve tiny leverets I disturb. There are two pairs of buzzards and a pair of kites keeping a watching brief over my activities. The leverets have a choice: run uphill over what I've cut, or downhill towards the wood. I agonise over the ones going uphill because there's no cover up there for a long way. The thistles form a sort of canopy and it would be almost impossible for a winged predator to penetrate the three feet or so of dense thistle to catch anything. Hares aren't so dull after all, breeding amongst the thistles. Except the ones that run uphill.

★★★

As the seasons progress through the year, the anecdotes progress in the pub, in a similar timely fashion. And as I sit there and listen, I note an element of one-upmanship that exists. That follows the seasons as well: who has got the biggest, the most, the earliest? I'm not sure when the anecdotal year starts, it doesn't follow the calendar year exactly, but it's not long into the New Year when the sheep farmers start scanning their ewes. This is a process a bit similar to scanning a baby still in the womb and identifies which ewe will have how many lambs. It's a useful management tool because ewes only carrying one lamb don't need as much extra feed as ewes with twins, for example. Ewes carrying single lambs may be left, on some farms, to lamb outside.

It's also useful to know if a ewe is carrying three lambs because the farmer can snatch one lamb away at birth and foster the lamb onto a ewe with a single. It's all good stuff to report in the pub and as the scanner man progresses around the area, crumpled envelopes are produced from crumpled jackets and scanning reports are given, digested by the assembled company, and suitable advice given. Not everybody shares this information: one farmer slipped me a piece of paper just a bit bigger than a postage stamp, 'That's our scanning.'

It was fascinating, knowing how many ewes he had. No one ever knew how many he had and here it was written down. I started to add the numbers up, he guessed what I was doing and snatched the paper back, I'd got to 2,000 and still had two more lots to add in, 'Don't you tell anybody.' Next in the season is the arrival of the first lamb, 'We had our first lamb yesterday,' 'How's it doing?' 'It's doing fine.' It would be fine because it's the only lamb they've got and will be hanging around the stackyard in the dry with its mother. It's the only lamb they've got because they don't really start lambing for another month, didn't he tell us that just about a few weeks ago when he told us about his scanning? It's the result of his tups getting out or he hadn't castrated one of last year's lambs properly, but no one is unkind enough to say that. A first lamb is a first lamb.

So we go on week by week. 'We put some fertiliser on today.' No one speaks and the original speaker feels isolated, but they've all noted what he's said and as I go about my business over the next few days I see most of them putting fertiliser on. I know a mischievous farmer in West Wales who was clearing a barn out to prepare it to bring the ewes in to lamb. Their fertiliser spreader was parked in the barn and they had to put it on to the tractor to move it out of the way. It was only an hour before lunch and although it was still January, he told his son to drive round and round the fields next to the barn with the empty spreader on to make it look as if he was in fact putting some fertiliser on. When they came out after lunch they could look down the valley and four farms had their fertiliser spreaders busy in the fields!

★★★

The year goes on and work and farming goes on, and all is duly reported in the pub. 'We cut some grass today for silage.' 'We cut some hay today.' 'Our winter barley is ready.' 'We'll start our wheat tomorrow.' Which brings us up to date. We've missed all the rain around here and are in the driest year we've had since '76. So someone suggests last night, 'If we had some nice warm rain, there'd be some mushrooms about.' 'It's too cold for mushrooms,' contributes another. He's dead right, it's pullover and fleece stuff in the mornings.

But here we go, 'Mushrooms, we've never had so many, there's little buttons everywhere, I leave them a couple of days to get bigger, couldn't get them all in the pan this morning.' This is a clear example of the one-upmanship I referred to earlier: it is so far towards exaggeration, it's probably all lies. I've got a good place for mushrooms and there's no sign of them. 'Where did you find them?' asks another. There's no answer to that.

The mushroom man continues, 'and puff balls, boy, they're good, a pan full of puff balls and then a pan full of fat bacon and two duck eggs.' 'I wouldn't eat puff balls,' is the general consensus but we are assured that if you can peel it you can eat it, 'and I eat that fungus that grows on the sides of trees.' There are reflective pulls on pints: they are quietly salivating about the mushrooms, but that's as far as most of us will go, we need a bit more science than 'if you can peel it you can eat it.' Many years ago I used to eat those huge horse mushrooms regularly, then one night I nearly died, well it felt like dying at the time. That was enough of a fungi adventure for me.

SEPTEMBER 17TH 2011

There's an area of land from Gloucestershire up through the West Midlands towards Cheshire where we have experienced a drought year that compares in severity with that of 1976. Fields everywhere are brown; our own fields have odd green patches in them in the damp places where you should really put a drain. It's a strange phenomenon because I have friends who live in Cumbria where it is so wet that they have had to keep their cows in at night.

Most farms are short of winter feed and it will be a real on-going problem unless we can take some late silage. Fodder and straw prices are already at record levels. If you keep beef cattle you have the option of selling stock but with dairy cows, well you just want to keep them. We'll come through this, we always have and always will, but for most dairy farmers in this area, these are extra costs we could well do without.

★★★

'Got a story for you.' The man, who I know well, has sidled up behind me. He looks furtively about to make sure no one else is listening. This is strange because I know that he is going to tell me his story in the full knowledge that I will pass it on to you. 'I've just bought a new Texel tup.' [A tup is a ram, but round here we call them tups.] 'It's a smart tup, paid a fair bit for him, and when I got him home I was well pleased with him. I've got him out in the orchard with half a dozen lambs for company and every day I take them some corn. I put the corn out in the trough and stood back to admire the tup, once again. The tup lifted his head out of the trough and turned to look at me, and a voice said, "Hello".

'Well, I didn't know what to think, I looked all about me, [I'd just seen him doing this, looking all about me, and he's quite good at it], there was no one anywhere about, so I looked at the tup and said "Hello" back to him. Again a voice said, "Hello."

'I thought to myself, "This is one hell of a tup I've bought here, it can talk to me," so once again I said "Hello" back to it.' "What the hell do you want?" came the voice again, but this time I knew it wasn't the tup because he'd got his head back in the trough and had a mouthful of corn. Then I realised I'd knocked my mobile phone in my pocket and inadvertently phoned someone.' And he goes off, but still looking furtively about him.

★★★

Most of the harvest frenzy has abated now. As far as I can tell, everyone has finished combining around here except for me and I've still got 20 acres of wheat to do. I call it frenzy because the roads locally were very busy for a month with tractors and combines going about their harvest business. There's quite a lot of corn grown where I live and a number of livestock farms just a tractor ride away, so loads of straw behind tractors are the most common sight. The odd bale becomes a casualty and falls off the load, but no matter, it's all part of the harvest pageant.

One pub regular lost four big square bales on one journey and is apparently so mortified at his incompetence that he hasn't been seen out socially for three weeks. If it's a big round bale that falls off, it can have a mind of its own and go walk-about. We call these 'runners'. Three fell off on the main street of a local market town, no one hurt, no damage done, and to be fair to the bales, they took a short journey down the hill and then parked themselves tidily amongst the cars.

In the village there's a bit of straw about in the gutters, and always a few wisps of straw in the air as a load makes its journey. You hear mutterings in the pub, 'Some straw on the road,' 'They ought to be made to sweep it up.' If you picked every fragment up, it wouldn't be enough to put around your strawberries. It's strange how one sector of society sees us farmers, with our hold-ups and our straw, as a damned nuisance, whilst we for our part think we are doing something very useful, gathering food.

★★★

I was at a presentation the other day where we were told that if the population continues to grow as it is presently growing for the next ten years and if food production is the same in ten years as it is now, then there just won't be enough.

It's a sobering statistic because there are millions of people who would say there isn't enough food now and millions more who exist on what we, with the food luxuries we enjoy, would say is a subsistence diet. As those ten years progress we will see food security climb to the top of the agenda and once again take its rightful place at the top of our daily needs.

But we're not 10 years down the line, we're 'safely gathering' in at this harvest. The loads of straw and grain are already being replaced by huge loads of potatoes, travelling at speed, driven by cool young lads wearing sunglasses. This is nature's bounty, a bounty that man has refined into the sophis-ticated operation it has now become. But there is also another bounty. The fields are full of berries, fruits, nuts and fungi that we can also enjoy.

A friend of mine always says that there is a month at this time of year when we could live well on what is available free in woods and fields. When I go about the farm there are people gathering blackberries, people tentatively gathering sloes from blackthorn bushes, (these are secret drinkers of sloe gin!) and I also do some gathering of my own. There's one track I drive where the hedgerow closes in on you as you drive along and it is a simple matter to reach out and gather, quite nonchalantly, some hazel nuts for your immediate consumption. I like that word nonchalantly, it describes exactly what I do, I pluck a few nuts and I put them on the seat next to me. And as I progress on my round I can take one nut at a time, pop it in to my mouth, crunch it, and enjoy the kernel inside. The last nut I crunched has just cost me £350 at the dentist so I don't do it anymore. The only nonchalance to be seen is from the dentist's receptionist as she took the money from me.

SEPTEMBER 24TH 2011

It's been windy here over the last few days. My wife reckons it's the tail end of hurricane Katia. She always reckons things like that. If they get exceptional weather in the States, she always says, 'We'll get it next.' I always disagree, it's an important matter of principle to disagree with your wife, but she's often right. We had to fold up the sheets on our silage pit before they disappeared to wherever the wind would take them. Of more concern is the damage to a cherry tree. When I came to live here my Dad bought and planted two flowering cherry trees and planted them in front of our house. The wind has taken half of one of them out. We can tidy up what's left with a chain saw but what's left is weakened considerably, and because my Dad planted the tree, it leaves me a bit sad.

★★★

A couple of months ago we had what we call the Dairy Event. So I'm sitting on our stand talking to dairy farmers and a man I don't know comes up, puts a piece of paper on the table with his name and phone number on, and says, 'I want a corgi pup like yours.' So I've sent his details to the corgi lady, who has just had another litter, and if he buys one, and if it is anything like mine, heaven help him.

★★★

It has been at the back of my mind for some time that, should I ever lose my driving licence to the breathalyser, I would buy a horse and cart in order to continue to go to the pub. I take some effort to make sure this doesn't happen, I usually drink either ginger beer or cranberry juice to start with, then I might have a couple of glasses of wine, and then in the hour before I actually go home, a pot of tea.

By the time I get to the tea, most of my friends in the pub are on their eighth pint and the pot of tea and milk jug and sugar causes some amusement. If the landlady is in a good mood I might get a couple of sandwiches to go with the tea. My abstinence is seen as a bit of a challenge and sometimes another glass of wine is bought and placed in front of me. There seems to be huge police activity around here at the moment, huge as compared to none, so you just never know. Before I progress this story, it may be of interest to you to know that both ginger beer and cranberry juice double in volume as they pass through your body, which is not a good thing if you want a good night's sleep.

★★★

I've given quite a lot of thought to the horse and cart idea. To start with, I wouldn't want just a horse; I'm too old now to fall off anything. My fantasy of riding up the main street of our local town dressed like Clint Eastwood in the film '*The Outlaw Josey Wales*' is just that now, a fantasy. My fancy now is a sort of shire horse with the kind of cart they would at one time have used to cart root crops, and we would plod our way to the pub, the horse and I, with me sitting on the side of the cart and we would appear like a spectre from a bygone age, and people would slow down to stare at us and the locals would say, 'He's a bit of a character.'

I know where I will keep the horse, though I haven't told my son, I know that I will be safe on the road because I will fit a battery to the cart so that I have lights and a flashing beacon, and

I'll be able to drink what I like because the horse will know the way home to its warm stable, where it will also know there will be food waiting for it, whatever it is that horses eat. It won't cost much to keep the horse because the landlady at the pub, apart from making excellent cucumber sandwiches, is a bit of a softy with animals and would probably buy some hay for it to eat while I am in the pub. So I've got this important element of my life sorted in my mind, but as usual, it's not new, nothing ever is.

Many, many years ago there was a farmer locally who would go by pony and trap to our local market every Friday. Farmer, pony and trap are now long gone, as you can imagine, but we also need to imagine how important this market trip would be within the social life of the time. He was from a lonely isolated farm, where you would only see your immediate family on normal days.

So I suspect it would be the highlight of his week and the pony would be groomed up smart and he would probably be wearing shiny leather gaiters and a collar and tie and off he would go. It wouldn't be a big market in those days, a few cattle, a few sheep, a pig or two, and once it was over he would drive the pony around to the pub, which would be open all day for the market, and where sales representatives would lie in wait.

And he would drink considerably from early afternoon until early evening. So considerably, that it was quite normal for him to be carried out of the pub and put in a heap in the trap, the pony untied, given a smack on the backend and off it would trot safely home. The farmer knew what would happen to him on market days and before he left in the mornings he would leave the stable door open and put a pile of sweet hay, a pony length inside the door. So when the pony returned home it would head straight for its stable and would go in as far as the wheels of the trap would allow and stay there quite content until the farmer woke up and could remove the trap and unharness the pony.

But that isn't quite the end of the story. The lads in a nearby village knew all about market days and drunken farmers and ponies in traps and they hid on his yard one evening. In those days, a country lad would go nowhere without a catapult in his pocket, and very proficient he would be with it; it was an essential in his life, bit like a hooded jacket today! So they waited for the pony and trap to return and just as the pony trotted up to the stable door it had a sharp stone hit it in the rear. It shot forward instead of slowing down, the trap wheels hit the doorposts, and both broke and threw him out onto his mucky yard. I don't expect this to ever happen to me: the shed I have in mind will allow the unimpeded entry of both horse and cart, and anyway, boys don't carry catapults anymore.

OCTOBER 1ST 2011

A previous tenant of most of the land I farm knows all the old field names. I intend to sit down with him one day and make a note of them all and then to start using them. If I refer to a field by its old name, it should only be a short time before they become used daily by all of us who work here. If they try to use the names we use now and I look at them, blankly, well they'll have to use the old name to make me understand; I think it will work. More importantly I will start to use the names with my grandchildren 'sowing the seed' for their use for another three generations. I often talk to you about my top land, which goes up to 1,000 feet; we presently call it the mast field.

Just over the hedge in the next field is one of those television masts that were built at a time when most of us who lived in hilly border areas enjoyed television pictures that were predominantly snowstorms with people walking about in the background. The mast field was apparently called Tottermans field - a totterman was the man who lived up there all the year round in order to light the beacon to warn the community if the Welsh were coming. It's a cold windswept place and it can't have been a pleasant place to live and if it was your job to watch for invaders, it was sure to be a bit scary. But if that was what you were told to do, and in the times when you were told to do it, well if you didn't do it, the consequences would have been a bit scary as well. The Welsh wouldn't be invaders really, because traditionally, around here would have been Wales. The original boundaries of Wales were the natural borders afforded by the Severn and the Dee, with just a short piece of border joining the two north of Shrewsbury.

I've got this huge dictionary that I rarely use because I can hardly lift it, and Totterman is not in there, the nearest word is totter, and we all know what that means. Next to Tottermans field is a field, not mine, called 'John's piece'. That's interesting isn't it, and worthy of investigation.

★★★

Autumn is one of my favourite times of year, not for colours and mellow fruitfulness, but because it's the time of year when people with greenhouses bring me all their surplus tomatoes. One of my favourite meals is fried tomatoes. I was worried about fried tomatoes this year because 'they' won't show me how you use the new ceramic hob on our new cooker. But as with my attempt to fry eggs in the microwave, I won't be beaten. One of the most contentious issues in our house is when to fire up the Rayburn in the autumn. This is my area of expertise and I often try to drag it out until mid-October. But you can fry tomatoes on a Rayburn can't you? So I quietly light it up one morning. 'Thank you for lighting the Rayburn for me.' 'That's OK.' I can smell the tomatoes frying as I write this.

★★★

At long last we've had some rain. It's been cold, but the grass is starting to turn green again; it's not growing, but it's changing colour, which is a start. And with the rain have come some mushrooms. Funny things mushrooms, they bring out the worst in people, including me. The first ones and I'm peeling them at the kitchen table, I've got the bowl well close to me with as much of my arms around the bowl as I can get, a bit like when I was at school trying to stop people copying my work.

A friend burst in to the kitchen and catches me with my mushrooms. 'Ooh, field mushrooms, where did you find them?' 'Not telling you.' Tell someone where you found mushrooms and your first meal will be your last, because they will pick them before you can and they will tell someone else and they will pick them as well and they'll both be looking for them in the same place next year so, 'not telling you' seems quite reasonable. 'I just love field mushrooms.' This is mushroom-speak for: you will have to give me some and if you don't, you are a completely selfish swine. So I look at my mushrooms and decide that four or five will have to go to this visitor, not happy, but what choice do I have? 'All our family love mushrooms.' Four or five times four is 16 or 20! My mushrooms are getting less by the minute and at the same time I'm left feeling as if I've done something wrong and I'm selfish and greedy. All I did was go around the cattle as usual in the morning, I noted the change in the weather, went to my best mushroom place, spent an hour wandering about looking for them and within an hour I'm on my back foot and feeling that I've done something wrong. I sort out about 15 mushrooms which is about half of what I've got. I take care to pick out the older ones with the unmistakable holes of grubs in the stems. Bring out the worst in people, mushrooms.

★★★

We went to a family party in mid-Wales on Sunday. It was on an isolated farm amongst the most beautiful wild scenery you can imagine. I take a break from the activities in the marquee to go outside to lean on a wall and to take in the wonder of it all. Then over the fields, out of the mist, I can see a young woman walking towards me. She has long auburn hair and long flowing clothes. There used to be an advert on television for an Irish beer where just such a beautiful young girl appears out of the mist. Her long skirts and white petticoats are wet from the long grass but her feet are dry because she's got wellies on. She comes up to me and puts her hand out in greeting, 'Hello, I'm Denise, I live down the dingle.' Just thought I'd share that with you. Wonder if she's got any company down the dingle?

OCTOBER 8ᵀᴴ 2011

Some of you who read this might be walkers so I will tread carefully amongst you. We have on our land, one footpath that is regularly used. It travels close to what I call our top land, which is a favourite place of mine. Although I go up there every day, I never cease to marvel at it all and am delighted that the footpath gives others the opportunity to do the same. It is used regularly by locals, who often pass comment on crops and livestock, and it is used in the summer by many visitors to the area. Local or visitor, I always stop for a chat, pass the time of day, and identify points of local interest, of which I am just one. Most walkers like to chat, but a few don't, and what intrigues me about the latter is that they appear to get more satisfaction from finding something wrong than they do from the actual walk.

There were a lot of walkers from the South East of England last week, I know that because I spoke to many of them, but as I went up and down the field on the tractor I noticed one small group who paused at each stile and gave it a good inspection including a good shake. Thought no more about it: each to his own.

But a week later I spot tyre tracks that I don't recognise going through a gateway, so I revert to my Apache mode and follow the tracks. Quite soon I find a 4x4 truck belonging to the county council. The driver tells me that they've just had some complaints about bits of stile being loose and they have to go up there and tidy them all up. Seems a bit strange to me, when costs are having to be cut everywhere, that someone from outside our area can insist on our council spending money.

There was a letter in our local paper next night calling for footpath expenditure to be exempt from cost-cutting. A big and important part of my life was spent at the rugby club on and off the field. I go down there four or five times a year to watch. First thing they say, 'Nice to see you down here,' and second, 'Can we have 50 quid for your subscription please?' So I have to pay for my recreation, but not, it seems, walkers.

★★★

In the pub. 'Nights are drawing in.' 'They are, be damned.' As if this is some new phenomenon! 'Soon be time to alter the clocks.' 'Which way is it this time?' Not that straightforward for me, altering clocks. I've rarely worked out how to alter clocks in the car. It's not that big a problem for me because I always know what the time is by adding or subtracting an hour either way, but for some reason it infuriates passengers.

One man who I used to work with, fidgeted away for a few miles before he came out with, 'your clock is wrong.' 'I know.' 'So how do you know what the time is?' 'By knocking off an hour.' 'But this clock is an hour and twenty minutes out, where did the twenty minutes come from?' 'They were doing a job on the car and had to disconnect the battery for 20 minutes' 'So if you want to know the time, you have to subtract an hour and twenty minutes?' 'Yes.' And he splutters and forces himself to look out of the side window. I know of two brothers who never altered their clocks or watches, just carried on the same, started with an hour different to everyone else, had their meals an hour different, finished work at different time. Every year people agonise about changing the clocks and ask should a change be permanent, but as these two brothers proved, there's only 24 hours in a day, so do with it what you will.

★★★

We had quite late frosts around here in the spring and they weren't just the touch of frost that comes at first light, they were minus 3's and 4's. Strangely they didn't affect the blossom or the subsequent fruit crops. There are areas near here where there isn't an apple to be seen, yet just around here the apples are a bumper crop and breaking branches. This autumn bounty has not gone unnoticed in the pub and heads have been together and there is much talk of cider-making. Some just talk about it, a bit like a lot of things in their lives – all talk and no action.

But there are others who are not like that, much more resourceful, who actually get things done, and it is these people who gravitate together and I can see by the way they have their heads together that they mean business. One evening, three of them nonchalantly pull stools up to where I'm sitting. 'You've got an old cheese press?' 'Yes.' 'Does it still work?' 'Yes.' That's me finished with, in the conversation. It is taken for granted that a cheese press will squeeze apples and it is also taken for granted that they can borrow it (which they can).

Although none of them have made cider before, they are all experts, and as I write I am conscious that there will be many cider experts amongst the readers of this book. 'My old granddad always said that to make good cider you had to hang a piece of fat bacon in it while it was fermenting.' This is interesting, because going back those three generations, cider would be made on all the farms around here. We have barrels in our cellar that are too big to go through the doors and were presumably assembled in the cellar.

The others aren't to be outdone on this piece of subtle cider-making. 'My granddad always said you should hang a piece of cheese in it.' It's the third one's turn now and he's not to be outdone, 'and a dead rat.' They contemplate this piece of information for a moment, 'I could supply the rat, we've got plenty at our place.' But they haven't forgotten the basics either. 'I know an old girl I do some gardening for her, she's got a cider orchard, she'll give me all the apples we need.'

So the conversation has apparently gone full circle, they've got the press, the apples, bits and pieces you have to hang in the barrel, job done. But it isn't. 'MY old granddad said that if you needed to put water in it, you got the water from the duck pond.' And I make a mental note that if I am ever given some cider for the loan of my cheese press, not to drink it.

OCTOBER 15TH 2011

So we passed our TB test last week which came as a surprise and left me with a feeling that I didn't know how I felt. My eldest grandson had his first hangover and says he will never drink again; he marked the occasion by being sick in the hedge while we were moving cattle for the TB test. He's just passed his driving test and it seems strange when he goes off somewhere and you don't have to take him or fetch him back. I went for my first long journey in my 'new' car and decided I would make it an Irish occasion and put all my Irish CDs in the cartridge in the boot. Bit disappointed when I accelerated in to the fast lane on the motorway, pushed the button and nothing happened. When I got home, I left the car unlocked in the pub car park, told the smokers about the problem; they had the boot open and sorted it for me in no time.

★★★

I keep wittering on about balance in nature or to be correct, imbalance, and no one takes any notice. So Stephen who works with us is ploughing some grassland up for winter wheat. We would have preferred to put the wheat in a bit earlier but the ground has been too dry and hard to plough until now. Even now it's only just ready to plough and it's a slow job: lose concentration and the plough is out of the ground. So he's ploughing away slowly and it's slow enough to count the birds that are following. He counts 34 buzzards and four red kites! No wonder there's fewer skylarks up there than there were five years ago: what chance do they have?

★★★

Up 'on the top' on the tractor, and two fields away a neighbour is trying to move some cattle. It's only a small group, a bull, a few cows and calves, all Limousin. They've been up here all summer, and it's quiet and isolated. The neighbour drives around them every day in his Land Rover so it could be that the calves, born up here, have never seen a human being on its back legs, as it were. He's not having much luck. He's got the dogs out but the cattle soon saw them off and now he's chasing them with the Land Rover up and down, up and down. I get off the tractor for a call of nature and I can hear him shouting and blowing the horn. After two hours he gives up and the cattle lie back down after their exertions. I could have given him a hand but even I am too young to die.

Next day he's back with reinforcements. There's the Land Rover (which is full of barking dogs). There's a tractor and loader with a big bale of straw on the front, for cattle pushing purposes I presume, and two men on foot. He must need to get them in for his TB test. I drive my tractor a bit slower so I can watch. For two hours they chase the cattle up and down, up and down, and when they look as though they might be winning and have got the cattle somewhere near the gate out of the field, the bull chases the men, up and down, up and down.

They eventually give up and the cattle once again lie back down after their exertions. Wonder what they'll do next? A tranquilliser dart? A machine gun? I don't tell anybody else this story in the pub, it's private business, but there's no need, because somebody else already has. No secrets around here.

It must be the rolling nature of the hills in Shropshire that makes it possible to see what everyone else is doing on their farms. This is particularly true when you are all busy on tractor work. You are going up and down the field all day and at different distances you can see your friends and neighbours doing the same. You are watching them and they are watching you. Closely. Stop in the middle of a field for half an hour and the mobile phone starts to go, 'What's gone wrong?' I'm as bad myself but I don't phone them up and I don't carry binoculars, which I think some of them do. So we are all busy ploughing and working land last week and the phone goes, 'Look at _____!' He's ploughing, we can all see him and his plough has broken in half. Well it hasn't really broken in half, it's worse than that, he's using a five furrow reversible and he's left the back four furrows behind. So he's ploughing up a long field and turning just one furrow, the rest of the plough is sitting in the furrow where he dropped it in the ground. Trouble is, he goes all the way to the end of the field before he notices. He gets some stick on Thursday at farmers' night in the pub. He can only take it with a smile. 'Thought she was pulling well all of a sudden.'

★★★

It has been a desperately dry summer here, but you've heard enough about that. A friend of mine has a suckler cow that is leaning well over a roadside fence to get a mouthful of fresh grass, and she keeps on leaning and one thing leads to another and she finds that with a bit of a jump she is out of the field and grazing the roadside verge. What we call grazing the long meadow. But the grass is greener on the other side of the road, as it always is, and once again one thing leads to another, and she ends up on the bonnet of a car. She's not hurt but the driver of the car is not best pleased and phones 999.

The police turn up at about the same time as the owner of the cow. The policeman doesn't see the funny side either. 'How did your cow get on the road?' 'It's people stopping to go into the field for a pee and leaving the gate open.' This excuse will usually suffice but as there is no sign of a gate in the vicinity the policeman is still suspicious. He decides to conduct further on-the-spot enquiries. 'Look, if you are going to ask all these questions, you'd better stand over there,' says the owner of the cow. 'I'm the policeman; you don't tell me where to stand.' 'Well, you can stand there if you want to but if you do, that dog is just about to bite you.'

October 22ND 2011

The rain we had last night has made for more change than we've seen for weeks. Grass has visibly grown overnight and I'm particularly looking at the crops we sowed a few weeks ago and which have been struggling ever since. The grass seeds are much greener than they were yesterday and I turn my attention to our stubble turnips. These are a critical crop for us this year. Sown after wheat crops on land that will carry spring wheat next year, they are what we call a catch crop, a bit of an extra crop squeezed in between two main crops. But because we have suffered from the effects of a drought year and are short of fodder for the winter, the scale of the stubble turnip crop will be critical to how we get through the winter.

So I drive across the 25 acres we have sown at 1000ft and note that the turnips too have benefitted from rain. They germinated soon after we sowed them and have been waiting for a good drink ever since. This is a big field by our standards and was historically three fields made into one by a previous tenant.

For perhaps 30 odd years it would have been continuous cereals but historically it would have been farmed very differently. This is high ground, the soil is good but not that deep and it needs proper farming. It needs organic matter for continuing fertility and in the past they knew exactly how to do this. Organic matter is muck and muck means animals and in my own way within the constraints of modern farming I am doing my best to emulate what my predecessors, all those years ago, used to do as a norm.

This field or these three fields would have in a simple rotation. Starting with a stubble, manure from cattle yards would be spread during the winter and into the spring. The field would be ploughed and a crop of swedes sown. Most of the swedes would be grazed *in situ* by sheep in the winter. No handy electric fences to move, but wire netting and wooden stakes to hammer in. The swedes would be finished by spring and the field would be ploughed and drilled with spring barley and grass seeds put in at the same time.

There would be plenty of clover in the ley which would fix nitrogen as it was successively mown and grazed. Ploughed again after possibly two years there would probably be a crop of winter oats before the cycle started again. Every step of the way in this rotation, fertility would be returned to the land. I can't farm like that - no sheep for a start - but my rotation includes two wheat crops and two years of grass. I take the trouble (if that's the right word), to take a lot of manure up there, but as I drive through the sparse turnip crop, willing it to grow, I am mindful that, with luck, I will have cattle grazing the turnips this winter and that will probably be the first stock out-wintered up here for more than a generation. My neighbours say that they can already see the difference I am making, and that in itself gives a quiet pleasure.

★★★

To tell a story, you need to introduce the characters. There's a farmer, beef, sheep, a bit of corn. A contented life and a contented lifestyle. He's well into his fifties, fairly comfortably off, largely because his aspirations are modest and his pleasures come from the well being of his stock, the land he farms, and the beautiful countryside in which he lives. He loves shooting and recently bought himself a new shotgun, his previous gun being inherited from his father. And like a child with a new bike, he can't wait to try it out. So one afternoon, most of his day's work done, he takes himself off up to the top end of his farm where he has a wood, to try the gun out by shooting a few pigeons.

The other participants in this story are newcomers to the local village, only been in the area for six weeks. I don't know where they came from but we'll say they are Londoners. They have moved to the area because they love the beauty of it all and are determined to enjoy that beauty by taking walks in it. So, unknown to each other, our farmer is at the top of the wood trying to shoot pigeons with his new gun and the newcomers are strolling along the bottom of it. A shot rings out, to the surprise of the walkers, and, as what goes up usually has to come down, the spent pellets come pattering down harmlessly around them. If you don't know anything about shooting and you are a Londoner and you don't know anything about the countryside, it is quite clear that someone is shooting at you. They get over the hedge and get down on their hands and knees and begin to crawl for safety. Again there is a shot and they can hear the pellets pattering down on the fallen leaves not far from them. There is terror in their crawling now and an urgency to it but they pause just long enough to phone 999 and tell the operator that there is a madman at large who is shooting at them.

Meanwhile at the top of the wood, our hero, for such he is, has shot two pigeons, is well pleased with his gun, and is disappointed that no more pigeons have appeared. He waits half an hour but then gives it up as a bad lot: there won't be any pigeons now that that helicopter is swirling about up there. So he puts his new gun into its new sling, pockets the two pigeons, lights his pipe and starts to stroll home. His progress is monitored by the police helicopter above him who report to the armed response team who have sealed off the village, told everyone to remain indoors and are now secreted in cover waiting to ambush him.

He comes out of the wood onto his first field and is told by a loud-hailer to throw his gun to one side and lie face down. He's not best pleased about this as the grass is wet but he can see about ten armed police looking at him over gates and hedges and they look very serious. He puts down his new gun carefully and lies down beside it. He is soon surrounded by policemen pointing guns at him, one kicks his new gun further away, he lifts his head to protest but his head is pushed roughly back down. Equally roughly his hands are pulled behind his back and he is handcuffed. He is pulled to his feet and we can only imagine the sort of conversation that ensued. An indignant farmer minding his own business, all those keen policemen full of adrenaline. A local policeman turns up to find out what has happened, 'What's the trouble, Tom?'

OCTOBER 29TH 2011

We've got a cockerel in the yard. We rear pullets for layer units in batches of 39,999. Very important number that. If you have 40,000 all sorts of things happen to you, so you don't go there. These pullets are brown and they will go on to lay brown eggs. I think they are a sex-linked cross which means the females have the colour of the father and vice versa. But occasionally you get a cockerel in there, and cockerels aren't wanted on layer units, bit unfair really, depriving hens of their conjugal rights, but no matter, we've got this cockerel. His name is Neville. I don't know why he's called Neville. Neville has a wife who is an escapee from the last lot of pullets so I suppose she's some sort of illegal immigrant. They live together quite happily; they roam the yard at will. But Neville has taken to attacking people as well. He's not attacked me yet but I can see he's thinking about it! Neville and his wife live at night in the shed where cows calve; the lights come on in the early hours, so anyone on calving duty can see at a glance if there's anything needing attention. If they do have to venture in to assist a cow, it's not that easy with the cow lying in front of you and you trying to help her to calve and an aggressive cockerel on your back trying to peck lumps out of you.

★★★

It's an interesting subject, the names we give to animals. I know a gamekeeper who always has a lot of working dogs. They give their dogs old-fashioned men's names, so it's quite amusing to meet a sweet spaniel puppy called Gordon and the puppy has a father called Adrian. We've just had to buy a 'new' bull. He's what they call a British Blue. It's not that easy to find what we want. We need a white bull with a blue nose to get 'blue' calves out of our black and white cows. If you buy a blue bull you get black and white calves which may be worth less money. So I buy this bull and am told he had been purchased originally from a sale at a smallholding. We put him in to the trailer and I'm told that the bull's name is Peter. Peter is in the shed with the cows due to calve. Which is where Neville lives. It's all quite complicated.

★★★

I'm feeling quite nervous. I'm in the showroom of a Jaguar main dealer. I've brought in my 'new' Jag for a service. I've brought it here because I bought it on e-Bay and if there's any bad news to be had; this is the place to find out. I'm nervous because the consensus in the pub is that this service will cost me more than the car, which they all think is very funny. I've to wait here while

they do what they call a 'health check' which will determine if
there is anything wrong with the car that needs attention above
and beyond the service itself.

As I sit here waiting for them to do this 'health' check, I
am bound to make comparisons with a visit to the doctors. As I
arrive at the doctors I have to use a touch screen to identify myself
(never mind the three receptionists behind the frosted glass). I
then go to the waiting room where a digital display tells me when
to go to my appointment. That is the first time I get to speak to
anyone who works there.

When I came into the car showroom three people said
'Good morning' before I even got to the reception desk. When
I get there they have my details ready, 'We were expecting you.'
I'm shown to a waiting room with nice seating, given a cup of
coffee and today's paper. The magazines on the table are current
as well: in the doctors the magazines are history lessons. Everyone
who passes says good morning and asks if they can get me another
coffee.

When they've done the check, they take me through and
show me a couple of bushes that will be fine for now but will
need replacing before the next M.O.T. The attention I get is polite
and efficient. They all call me Sir, even though there's a pile of
farmyard debris on the floor under the ramp where my car is. (I
notice the other Jags don't have this pile). Calling me Sir makes
me nervous as well; usually the only people who call me Sir have
transit pickups with chrome wheels and want to know if I've got
any scrap. They begin the service. If I'm ever reincarnated as a
car, I hope I'll be a Jag. It's all very impressive. Might come to the
showroom next year for my flu jab.

Winter

NOVEMBER 5ᵀᴴ 2011

Because it's been so dry and because we are so short of fodder, we are trying to stretch the autumn into what will soon become winter as much as we can. But just like the tide, we cannot halt the inevitable. The cows at the moment are on the full winter diet that they have been eating for several months now (because of the dry weather). They go off down the fields for a stroll every morning and at nights they have the option of lying in the sheds or out in a nearby field. The numbers that lie inside varies according to the weather. We have to bring 30 heifers inside next week and that in itself marks the start of the increased winter workload. It's a workload that changes our daily routines, not least because it means a full day's work at weekends. I spend a lot of time trying to locate various winter garments that served me well in last winter's cold weather but were discarded one by one as spring arrived.

★★★

I've not heard of an organisation called Songbird Survival before (SBS). But I have in front of me a copy of a submission they have made to DEFRA. (Department of Environment, Farming and Rural Affairs). SBS describes itself as a charity dedicated to stopping the decline in the songbird populations. I think that I can confidently say that we're all up for that. The submission states that it is concerned about the effects of an increased level of badger predation on farmland birds. It highlights a recent study of 28 skylarks' nests, in which eight were predated, five by badgers.

They raise concerns about the effect of a 400% increase in badger populations over 40 years on ground-nesting birds, hedgehogs and bumble bee nests. They are concerned that the media and celebrities are mobilised to prevent any control of badgers regardless of the damage the growing numbers of badger can do to our ecosystems. It's a telling indictment that they cite the RSPB as absent from any forums suggesting the control of badgers, because such a stance could have an adverse effect on their membership and legacy income.

Half a billion pounds a year are spent on agri-environment schemes which deliver few benefits. The land I farm is in a scheme that costs thousands of pounds a year (not for me!) but there are fewer skylarks there than five years ago. In that time I've not seen a pair of lapwings nest there. I've highlighted this often enough, have spoken to RSPB people about it, have wondered why they are in denial about issues like the badger and winged predators like buzzards and magpies, and it seems likely that when it comes to the crunch, it all comes down to money.

It had always confounded me that the adverse affects of too many badgers and birds of prey, which are so obvious to me in my everyday life, could not be recognised by organisations like the RSPB for example. I attributed it to some sort of tunnel vision or a head in the sand attitude, but it seems the answer was there in front of me all the time: income is more important than principles, more important, apparently, than the birds it should protect. Somehow I expected better.

★★★

I embrace new technology as best I can. I think, for example, that a text is just, if not more, as effective as an email, if only because if someone hears their mobile phone 'ping' in their pocket, they are usually so nosy that they can't resist having a look to see what the text says.

For some time I have been in love with the actress Julia Roberts, (and I know that she has a feeling for me from the way she looks at me from the screen). Now that my daughter has taught me how to use the pin number on the TV remote control, Julia and I meet up more often. I also read my emails and sometimes succeed in making a reply.

Today I'm in the middle of a 20-acre field. It's largely brown with odd bits of green; there's been nothing in this field since the first week of July when we put three cwts to the acre of fertiliser on it. I'm on the mobile to a colleague, trying to explain how serious the drought has been in a strip of countryside that stretches from Gloucestershire up the Welsh borders almost to north Wales. I end the call with a sense that he hasn't believed me. Then I realise that I can do better than this, I can send him a photograph. I rarely use the camera on my mobile phone but it's there in my pocket and I get it out and photograph the desolate scene and send it to him. He's soon back on the phone wanting to know why I've sent him a photograph of my eye.

★★★

There's a road a couple of miles from here that is very minor in the scheme of things. It runs between two hamlets that are about three miles apart. I'm not sure if 'hamlet' is the correct word, as one of these comprises just four homes. Much of the road runs quite steeply through some forestry commission woods. The woods stretch for some distance either side of the road and are quite dense and dark. They are larch woods and some of the trees on the side of the road are also deciduous. Because the road is so narrow, the trees, larch and deciduous, contrive to touch over the road so for some distance you drive through a dark tunnel. It's the sort of drive that many years ago, I would have told my small children that there were Pogles in this wood, and they would have kept quiet for a while, while they nervously scanned the trees. Don't you know what a Pogle is? They turn up in the woods after teddy bears have had picnics.

Anyway one of the deciduous trees has a low-ish bough that stretches right across the road. Nailed to the trunk is a notice that says 'Boot Sale', and festooned across this branch (in the middle of nowhere) are about 50 boots and shoes dangling by their laces. No one knows who puts them there but the number continues to grow. So what's that all that about? It takes time and trouble, not least the trouble of preserving anonymity. The collection of boots and shoes doesn't look unsightly. I quite like it. It must be the work of an eccentric and I like eccentrics.

NOVEMBER 12TH 2011

I never stray, in my writings, into politics. Not my job, each to his own. But, regardless of a change of government, I thought there was a general consensus that we'd all had enough of bureaucrats affecting our daily lives. The ultimate example is Health and Safety. Most things that affect our lives have a pendulum and with Health and Safety that has swung from common sense to the clearly ridiculous. Against this background I was quite surprised to receive, some months ago, a form requiring me to register the fact that I had a septic tank. There must be thousands and thousands of us living in the countryside with septic tanks. Ours has been there for over 40 years that I know of and it wasn't new then, not by a long way.

It's not done anyone any harm, but you can just visualise how it all develops. You register it and then in the fullness of time someone comes to have a look at it and to justify their role, looking at septic tanks, they recommend some changes to it or even a new one, and so it goes on and on. More investigators, more cost.

I was at a party a few weeks ago and about eight farmers were sitting around the table discussing this very issue. All of them had already thrown their septic tank forms in the bin. This was very reassuring because that's what I had done. That won't be an end to it, merely a delaying tactic, but it's not the end of bureaucracy either. Now we are expected to register if we have a private water supply and that's not the end of that either. Because in the fullness of time the water will have to be tested as to its suitability for human consumption, a test that could cost up to £500. The people implementing this new requirement excuse their activities by saying that they are just complying with an EU directive, which is almost certainly true, but there is something in the makeup of the British bureaucrat that makes him climb all over this with enthusiasm whereas I suspect his French counterpart will give a Gallic shrug, leave it all to next year (in the hope that next year will never come) and fill another glass of red wine.

An awareness of this drinking water issue has filtered into the pub. We've all got private water supplies of varying degrees of sophistication. They are mostly supplied from springs and gravity-fed and as long as water comes out of the tap, they receive little attention. 'We found a dead mouse in our well the other day.' 'How long had it been dead?' 'Difficult to say. Should be OK to drink the water though.' The consensus is that the water is OK to drink as long as the mouse didn't have dirty feet when he fell in.

There's some 'newcomers' on the next table listening to what we are saying: they lower their heads together and I can tell they are appalled. I know a farmer who found two dead grey squirrels in the header tank in his loft, who cleaned the tank out and drank lemonade for six months. The 'fit for human consumption' bit is also a red herring. It's not unknown around here for some old person to die in their nineties, having lived in their isolated cottage for 50 years or so, enjoyed robust health all their lives until their bodies just got tired, drank the same water out of a spring all those years. The cottage is sold, the new owners have the water tested and it's not fit for humans to drink!

It's all double standards anyway. When I was a boy working on a farm, the boss was putting a piped water supply in. In those days you could get grants for this sort of work, but your water had to be 'fit for human consumption'. There were eight of us drinking this water with no ill-effects but it wouldn't pass the test. So he takes the sample bottle down to the village and fills it out of the tap of a house on mains water, sends it in as his own, and that fails as well! So he tells 'them' what he's done, they suggest he sends another sample of his own water and, surprise, surprise, it passes easily. Mains water wouldn't be fit for human consumption either if they didn't stuff it with chlorine. If I put chlorine in my milk there would be hell to pay. A lady from the water authority called here one day saying she was checking customer satisfaction on water quality. I asked of her if they piped it directly out of the local swimming pool because when I fill the kettle in the mornings I can smell the chlorine in the water. And filling up the kettle early in the morning is what I'm about to do now.

★★★

We brought some cattle indoors this week. They had to be loaded in a field and carted three miles to their winter housing. It's quite a big job because we have to corner them up, five or six at a time, in a gateway and there's lots of things can go wrong (and they usually do). No sophisticated loading pens, just a couple of gates and lots of string. There's two of us needed on this job and it occurs to me that if we had two stock trailers on the go, we would do the job twice as quickly as with one. This is the sort of innovative thinking that sets me apart from lesser mortals. We've got a couple of 4x4 trucks of a sort so I decide to try a long shot; I ask a neighbour if I can borrow his new stock trailer. 'Of course you can, it's on the yard, help yourself.' This response comes as a surprise but it's good news. 'You'll bring it back tonight won't you? We've got some lambs going to market in the morning, you'd better wash it out as well.' 'Of course I will.' First time we drop the ramp down we find the sheep decks are down and decks and floor are carrying about 6-inches of sheep poo! No wonder we could borrow the trailer, he just wanted it washed out.

★★★

I need to speak to the vet so I go into his office. He's deep into a huge textbook and he's got a big lizard-looking thing on his desk. Could be an iguana or something they call an exotic pet. I look the lizard over as the vet continues reading. 'Quite rare around here, lizards like that' I tell him. He doesn't look up from his book, 'They'll be rarer still if I get the operation wrong!'

NOVEMBER 19TH 2011

Talking of nature's abundant autumn harvest, a friend of mine reckons you could live quite adequately on the nuts and berries that are to be found in the fields and woods here in autumn. Judging by the size of his waist, he hasn't actually tried it for himself. Yesterday I found as many mushrooms as I have ever found at one time and never so many in November. I picked for a couple of hours and dispersed them around about six households. I put some of mine in the freezer.

But there's one harvest I forgot about. For weeks now I have been juggling scant grass growth, grazing cattle and declining water supplies, and after we put 30 cattle inside for the winter, we were able to move the few that were left out onto fresh fields. The harvest I forgot was acorns. I only remembered it when I spotted eight young cattle grazing tight together under an oak tree. If cattle are in a field all the time they cope quite well with acorns as they fall. If they've not been in a field for some time there will be an accumulation of fallen acorns that they will eat with relish. Too many and you are looking at upset stomachs and cattle very off-colour. Lots too many and you are looking at death. I've always known this but you can easily be preoccupied and busy and you can forget. My young cattle were fine.

***

Recently I had a rare Sunday afternoon off and went to a charity lunch. They are not a rare occurrence around here but there's something that seeps into a dairy farmer's conscience that tells him not to go out at lunchtime on Sundays if he has to be present at milking time. If you have to drag yourself out to milk at 3pm it's a much easier task if you are at home already, compared with coming home, probably later than you meant, but certainly before everyone else at the function, getting changed and then off out. Sunday lunchtimes are for sleeping in your armchair before you gather your resources to go out and milk cows once more. We used to have a village blacksmith who milked about ten cows who always reckoned that you should never go off for the day unless it was too far to come back to milk. There's an undeniable logic to it that I can empathise with and for years when I was doing most of the milking, I wouldn't go off for the day if I had to milk.

So I went out to lunch, lots of farming people there, people that I see from time to time but not often all together. It was a bit like a young farmers' dance with 50 years added to it. Too many old people there (of my age). It was the day the clocks went back, if they'd gone forward I don't think some of them would have made it.

***

There's a man on the phone, says he's coming to repair our TV. He asks for the postcode, pauses whilst he is presumably pressing buttons, then says 'I'll be with you at 12.17, is that convenient?' 12.17 what's all that about? How things have changed. And my mind is racing, reflecting on the change. We used to have a proper TV repair man who used to drive about in a little A40 that was stuffed with televisions. He smoked continuously; I can only remember that because he could smoke a whole cigarette without removing any of the ash, which I, as a non-smoker, thought quite remarkable.

He had a little shop where he kept dozens of televisions undergoing repair, and a long-suffering wife. He had so many televisions awaiting repair that he couldn't get into the shop in the morning for them until he had put some outside on the pavement, never mind that on some days it was raining. He put them all back inside at the end of the day. If your television broke down he would come and fit new valves and it would usually work. If it didn't, he would ferret about in his car and produce a TV that he would lend you, 'to tide you over'. He lent us one once for ten years and then he sold us a new one. You never ever took your TV to his shop because you would probably never see it again. There was none of this 12.17 stuff with him, if he was with you for an hour, most of that would be for talking.

He once told one of my favourite stories. A customer phones up and says he wants a new television. (I forgot to tell you this was at the time of a general election). So our man says 'but your TV is only six months old, I'll come and have a look and see if I can repair it.' 'I want a new television, bring one out.' The conversation sequence is repeated but the customer won't be put off, he has to have a new TV. The repair man won't be put off either, he puts a new TV in his car but he also puts in all the valves and paraphernalia that he is ever likely to need to repair a TV.

He goes out to the customer's home and is taken into the lounge. As soon as he enters the door he can see the TV screen is smashed. He goes up for a closer look, through the broken glass of the screen, and there, nestling amongst all the valves and bits and pieces, which are also smashed, is a gin bottle. He carefully takes his spent cigarette out of his mouth and puts it and all that ash in an ashtray. Lights up another and says, 'What you want here is a new TV.' He never told me who the customer was but, secretly, I've always admired him, haven't we all longed at some time to throw something at the television, haven't we all longed at sometime, to throw a gin bottle at life?

★★★

So what have an A.I. man, a tyre fitter and a machinery salesman got in common? Come to that, what have the postman and the man who reads the electric meter got in common? The former are hated by my dog, Mert, and the latter are almost licked to death in an effusive welcome. Causes some amusement actually, the A.I. man comes most days and tries to make friends. He came yesterday, went into the yard to do his work, Mert scowling at him all the time. When he'd finished, Mert wouldn't let him back out and he had to use his mobile phone to get help. The meter man comes just once a quarter and is greeted like a long-lost friend. It has always intrigued me how Mert makes his choices in his life and I can't work it out, but it keeps all our visitors on their toes.

NOVEMBER 26TH 2011

Remembrance Day last Sunday, and I was asked to 'say a few words' at a lunch in aid of the church afterwards. So I told the story of an old friend and employee who had worked on a farm during the war and one day 'they' turned up and gathered the five employees up together and said one of them had to join the army. Jack was the only single man there and they all looked at him, so off he had to go. He hated it. We often used to drive together past the camp where he was sent and he never failed to tell me how much he hated it, 'up and down that bloody parade ground all day long and then twice a day with full kit we had to run to that wood and back.' One day they got them on parade and said, 'Step forward any man who would like to earn an extra 2/6 a week.' Jack decided anything would be better than this and stepped forward. Not many weeks later the 2/6 earned him the right to jump out of a plane over Arnhem.

Just once, and we spent countless hours together, he told me that he spent three days in a wood that was being constantly shelled and one night he slipped quietly down the river bank and swam with the current several miles to get back behind Allied lines. The river was constantly sprayed with machine gun fire. We can hardly imagine the terror of that swim and the effect it would have on his life. Survivors of Arnhem were taken back to the UK and he had to help guard some German prisoners of war on the ships home. He befriended one and shared his cigarettes with him. Life is full of coincidences.

That farm where Jack worked is the farm I rent now and I often wonder if his 'work' is still there. Did he plant a tree, plant a hedge, help to put up a building? I'll never know now but it doesn't really matter because I remember him, I remember how proud he was of his Red Beret and remembering was what last Sunday was all about. But the coincidences keep coming. The German POW turned up locally to work on a farm. He never went home and I met him on the street of our local town last week. It makes you ponder how people can live harmoniously together who had previously fought, and what the point of it all had been?

It was a beautiful sunny autumn day here that Sunday. I drew my audience's attention to how lucky we were in our lives, to live amongst such beautiful countryside within a friendly community with its shops, church, school, pub. All the things that we often take for granted. But it is only when we stop occasionally and value what we are lucky enough to enjoy, all of that, and the comfort of our families growing up and the joy for some of us of our grandchildren, it's only when we stop to value all of that, that we can possibly begin to value all the sacrifices made by all of those who lost their lives on our behalf.

★★★

There's an old character lives in the village. He's in his eighties and he's telling me that when you turn 80 you get £400 a year winter fuel allowance. But they've only sent him £300 this year.

He's fairly philosophical about it, 'I've just worked it out, they think I'm going to die the first week in February.'

★★★

This is a delicate subject but in my efforts to be candid with you as I report on the incidents in my life and what I see around me, I feel obliged to carry on with this story. It concerns our new bull, Peter. Peter, you may remember, is what they call a British Blue, a breed that originated in Belgium, where it was called a Belgian Blue. We should all pause here to acknowledge the imagination of people who thought of this new name. Peter will breed us beef cross calves out of our dairy cows that will hopefully be worth good money. Peter is a young bull and when you buy a young bull you are told by the vendor that he has never worked. Work is the key word here and the word that takes us into delicacy. I will probably use this word several times before I finish this piece but what we are talking about is procreation or in our case, love-making. You may find it strange to describe love-making as work and some of you may even be thinking of going to the job centre looking for a career change but if that's what you bought him for and he doesn't do it, well it hasn't worked out, has it?

So Peter spent a week with us before he had the chance to do any 'work' and he lived quite contentedly with a few cows that were due to calve. At the back of your mind there is the thought that there might be a very slender chance that he won't work. But he had plenty of opportunity to study work because on wet days, Neville the cockerel spends a lot of time in the same shed with Lucy his wife. I don't think they are properly married but there's a lot of that going on these days. Peter had plenty of time to study work because Neville is working all the time.

So the day eventually arrives when there is an opportunity for Peter to work. It happens to be with a Jersey cow, which is quite convenient because, as work goes, it wasn't a big job. Despite having an audience that included Neville, Peter worked. No hesitation, job done. (Neville obviously hadn't taught him about romance.) Since then he's worked several times. And to be fair he enjoys his work, he enjoys it so much, he goes looking for it. He pushes open gates, he knocks down barriers, so dedicated has he become. The vendor said he hadn't worked, but he has now.

DECEMBER 3RD 2011

We have a diners club that meets in the pub in the village once a month. Sounds a bit grand, diners club, but it's not at all. We get two courses for £10 and the menu focuses on local traditional dishes whenever possible. Last month, for example it was beef stew and dumplings followed by rice pudding with skin on it and raspberry jam. There's usually 25-30 of us there and on one occasion a lady I don't know but who I've seen about the village sits down next to me. She's a bit older than me whereas I was hoping for something a bit younger but that's life and we start a conversation. She has an almost aggressive style and demands to know what I do for a living.

I tell her I'm a dairy farmer. She 'doesn't approve of dairy farming,' she tells me. 'Know a lot about dairy farming do you?' 'I certainly do, you keep your cows in dark dirty sheds all the year round, they never see the sun, never get to graze grass, they live short painful lives are exploited so that they have to calve every year, the calf is taken away at birth and shot, and as soon as the cow fails to make you any money, you shoot her as well.'

She draws breath, 'The only way the cow will survive is if you inject her with antibiotics every day.' It's interesting stuff. I disregard the stuff about the cows' life because I've seen her drive past our farm and cows have been out in the fields lying in the sun, so if you are blind enough not to want to see, well, that's her problem. The part that irritates me is the bit about antibiotics. It's something that I've come across before, quite a widely-held misconception. The reality is that a sample is taken from my milk every day and held for several days. It is routinely tested for quality and constituents and antibiotics. But the tanker is tested every day as well before it is unloaded and if there are antibiotics in the load it is a relatively simple task to visit the samples and find out where the contamination came from and the farm responsible has to pay for the loss of the whole load and its disposal. So if you were giving your cows antibiotics every day, you can't sell any milk. Simple!

So I manage to ignore my neighbour at the dinner table as best as I can and it works quite well because she is ignoring me because I've told her what she's said is disgraceful. Then the coffee comes around and I offer her the milk jug, 'Milk in your coffee?' 'Yes, please.'

★★★

Last week there was a piece in our daily paper about the causes of cancer. I'm turning the pages but stop when I see the word 'chicken'. Chicken, I am told, 'is full of the hormones widely-used in battery farms to promote growth. It will raise levels of oestrogen in humans which is associated with breast cancer.' But not to worry, you'd have to eat two chickens every day to increase your risk. Just how disgraceful and irresponsible a piece of journalism is that?

When I was a youth I had to earn all my pocket money, on farms, serving petrol, (remember serving petrol?), but I also kept about 20 hens and sold the eggs and once a year I had riches beyond belief, 12 cockerels for Christmas. Cockerels were challenging. Because the market was for large birds for Christmas dinner you had to cope with their sexuality and aggression. It was life in the raw, there were constant fights, gang rapes and inevitably one bird would be weaker than the rest and if left, it would be killed and there would be cannibalism. Bit like around here on a Saturday night.

But there was a simple solution; we would administer two small pellets under the skin. It was a dose of female hormone. It was administered under the skin of the neck as close to the head as you could get it. It was put there just in case the pellets didn't work and remained there, the idea being that that was a place least likely to be eaten by a human. The process was called caponising.

Quite soon after the birds were caponised, the aggression would go, their combs would disappear and they would get down to eating and growing, which they did very well, some of them growing as big as small turkeys. Male birds in a modern broiler system grow as quickly and are ready for the table so young that this aggression is never a problem. I'm not sure about the timing but hormones in meat-production was banned 20–30 years ago so to read of it this week as if it is still happening is just terrible. If someone said Roger Evans' chickens have hormones in them, I could take them to court but to say hormones are in chickens is apparently OK. And because it's apparently OK, people can slander a whole industry and get away with it.

DECEMBER 10ᵀᴴ 2011

A friend of ours has a new partner that we met for the first time recently. Really nice chap and we are finding out about each other. And he says he's not met many farmers but those he has are always moaning. There's a lot of truth in that. It probably needs some perspective: we have, for example to deal daily with the vagaries of the weather. Everybody else does too, but if the weather stops other people getting to work it becomes main headlines but on an almost weekly basis, the weather stops us getting our work done. As I write this, the television is showing a video of someone's dog chasing a deer in a London park. We livestock farmers have to deal with that sort of stuff on a daily basis.

The ingenuity of animals to contrive to do something negative is beyond belief. There's two ways to approach this sort of thing: I relate the story, I share it with you and I share it with other farmers down at the pub. I always try to bring out the irony and the humour of what has gone wrong. A lot of farmers find that upbeat approach difficult and inadvertently victimise themselves, hence the 'moaning farmer' label. It's probably a more serious issue than they realise. One of the things they moan about is the shortage of young people coming into our industry but if you are a young person, possibly from a farming family or with an interest in farming, and all you hear is people already involved in agriculture moaning about it, well, eventually you will get the message!

We've had a near-to-crippling drought this summer, certainly as bad as anything we experienced in 1976. Couldn't do anything about it, so no good moaning about it. Best, as always, to try to make the best of it. So we've just had the mildest of Novembers and ironically with most of the cattle inside for the winter, we have more grass than we've had for six months.

Our grazing area for the milking cows has so much grass that if it were May (if only) there would be enough grass for 150 cows for a month. But I don't start moaning about it, I go and get a bunch of in-calf heifers and turn them out on it. If the white stuff keeps away, this grass could last them until Christmas. Similarly I have 30-odd dry cows up to their knees in a grass crop that are not therefore eating away at silage stocks, which are very short because of the drought. So it's all looking better at the moment. When we moved the in-calf heifers, we used two 4x4s and two trailers. A tidy 4x4 and a tidy trailer and a similar outfit that would best be described as very tired.

Naturally I drove the best, and naturally I went first. When we got to where the heifers were, Stephen says 'Did you see that car?' 'What car?' I've told you, I'm sure, that it's a bit scary pulling out onto the main road out of our lane, mainly because the traffic is so fast. Apparently I pulled out first and there was a man approaching out of nowhere about 200 yards away, what Stephen describes as a rally car doing possibly 100mph, who overtakes the van in a bad place in the road, gets back on the right side of the road and sees my trailer about 50 yards in front of him. Slams on his brakes and spins into the hedge. The hedge is OK but there were lots of bits of plastic on the road, shame about that. Wouldn't have happened if we hadn't had an autumn flush of grass.

★★★

My mornings follow a fairly regular pattern. I get up early and do some writing and drink lots of tea. Some breakfast at eight o'clock and then, usually, some phone calls. Because I use my mobile for most of my phone calls I have to move out of the kitchen where the signal is very indifferent and into our sitting room where it isn't. On the settee by the window is the best place, so I'm sitting there on my fourth or fifth phone call and the other member of the household passes through.

They say a woman's work is never done, but if they got up a bit earlier in the mornings there might be a chance of getting it finished. Moving quickly on, it's only a few moments before I hear, 'What the hell have you been doing in this kitchen?' There is a blame culture in our house: if anything goes wrong, I get the blame. The most contentious issue in our house are the lights in our sitting room, they are a sort of cluster, designed, I imagine, to resemble candles. They go 'pop' at quite regular intervals as you switch them on. As each one goes, the light the cluster affords obviously gets dimmer, but that's not the whole story. When a bulb goes, the electricity trips out on two fuse boxes and the emergency lighting we have for the B&B comes on. And I don't know how to switch it off. Angry words are often exchanged over these lights and I want something different.

But it's apparently my fault that they go 'pop'. 'You switch them on too quickly.' I pause here for a second while I give you chance to consider the absurdity of that accusation. But let's get back to the here and now. What's happened in the kitchen? I do a quick recall. The marmite and spread are back in the fridge, the plate and knife are in the sink. The mug I've been using is in my hand. Can't think of anything else that could be an issue. I complete my phone call but in the distance I can hear angry mutterings, so I go to face the music.

Our oil-fired Rayburn has had what is best described as a blow-back. A sort of indigestion, a sort of oily, sooty belch. Obviously this is my fault. If ever you delve into the inside of an oil-fired cooker you find masses of black sooty stuff but it's got an oily smeary property to it. The Rayburn and everything within a yard of it is covered with this. The floor, the cooker itself and some tea towels drying on the top of it and some clothes drying on the rail. Order is soon restored but that's not the whole story. Something else spends a lot of time nestled against the comfort of the Rayburn. Our corgi. Today we have a black corgi. She's licked most of it off now. Yuk! So we have a corgi that looks like a meerkat with a black head. Could have been worse. Could have been me.

DECEMBER 17ᵀᴴ 2011

I've raised my own doubts about the benefits to wildlife of some of the conservation work that goes on. I always identify balance as the main issue because I see, for example, the wide proliferation of predators as a huge barrier to growth of songbird populations. I was taking a load of barley straw for our heifers to eat, at buildings we rent, and the sky seemed to be full of buzzards swirling about on the wind. Where I was is an estate with a large commercial shoot and despite their best efforts, I'm sure the odd uncollected bird is not picked up by the dogs and is eventually hoovered up by the buzzards and other predators.

'They' are trying to extend the proliferation of red kites in mid-Wales into England. Red kite feeding stations are apparently stopping the birds spreading because they stay near this abundant food supply and don't continue their move eastwards. I know many people in mid-Wales who think there are too many kites about and the numbers take them into the nuisance bracket, and you hear similar reports from the Chilterns.

We see kites all the time now; two or three years ago, rarely. No one seems to ask if anyone wants these birds to spread and increase in numbers. I've not heard of anyone asking the skylarks and lapwings and other ground nesting birds what they think about it. But I began this piece by talking about the conservation work done, at huge expense, which does nothing to stem the decline of farmland birds. There was a report on this the other day that backs up what I've been saying for a long time. Predation was flagged up as a huge barrier to songbirds staging a comeback.

But there is one success story, which is the margins: because two metres compulsory, six metres in environmental schemes, are a haven, amongst the tussocky grass, for all sorts of mice. And if it's good for mice, it's good for owls. I have no proof of this but from my own observation I think that there are more owls about. I like owls, and in particular I like barn owls. If you ever get up close to one, possibly one that's been through a taxidermist's hands, did you ever see anything with such beautiful feathers? I won't try to describe them because the intricacies of the patterning is beyond my descriptive powers, but what a beautiful bird. The downside for barn owls has been their habit of hunting along the grass verges of roads, mainly because they hunt at car height, and that has taken a huge toll on them over the years. I've always thought that some could be avoided: a white bird in the headlights is not difficult to spot, but if there is a car coming the other way at the same time, perhaps it's not so easy. So if there is a six-metre margin of conservation strip the other side of the hedge and the owl can hunt safely, well that's great.

★★★

As I join my fellow farmers in the pub, one of them has his trouser leg rolled up. It's not a pretty sight and I hope, fleetingly, that he doesn't progress to taking his socks off. Don't need to go there. The centre of everyone's attention is an angry red mark on his calf muscle, about two inches in diameter. The mark, he tells everyone, is the result of an attack on him by Neville, our free-range cockerel. The mark is all the more remarkable because it was inflicted through his welly! There's a lane runs through our yard, it's a council lane that is well overgrown and only used by 4x4s and tractors. He is, in theory our next-door neighbour along this lane, even if he lives a mile away.

One of our enterprises is to rear pullets that go away from here at 16 weeks of age to free range egg laying units. When these pullets are being caught, we sometimes get escapees that we eventually gather up and sell wherever we can. This is the retail side of our business, and we are talking here of possibly ten pullets a year! Neville is here because he wasn't a pullet. So this neighbour buys his wife four of these point-of-lay pullets for her birthday and it was when they came to collect them that the attack took place. 'Look what your cockerel did to my leg,' he says. 'Just shows what a soft life you have up that lane,' I tell him. 'You enjoy the soft under-belly of life; down on our yard we live life in the real world, life in the raw and if the cockerel doesn't get you, the dog will.'

DECEMBER 24TH 2011

It's Sunday morning, it's not that early but it's not been light for very long. I've been around the dry cows that we still have out and I'm about to drive up to our very top field where we have 25 acres of stubble turnips. These went in after a crop of wheat and I have set great store on these turnips to grow into a good crop that I can graze in January with dry cows and in-calf heifers thus replacing scarce silage stocks that I don't have because of the dry summer. These turnips germinated well, the plants are all there but they're not bulking up.

But ever hopeful, I drive up there once a week to have a look. There's a stone track to drive up. On one side is a game crop of about an acre for the pheasants with several wheat feeders dotted about in it and on the left, the boundary hedge to the next estate. This is about the time of day, when, if the syndicate were shooting, they would be sending some beaters out to the boundaries to keep the pheasants in these game crops for when the guns arrive.

I stop the truck. The track in front of me is alive with pheasants. I count over 50 and stop. They are all making their way up the track, not in a huge hurry but also with some purpose. I follow very slowly and the procession continues up the track for about 400 yards and then they start to file through a hole in the hedge, across a wheat crop to where there is a small group of fir trees about 200 yards away. So I start to put their day together thus far in my mind. Up at first light from the trees where they roost, into the game crop for a good breakfast of wheat and then, as I witness now, up the track on to the next estate and the sanctuary of these trees and the briars and thorns that grow beneath them.

And is it my imagination running away with me, or is this not all planned perfectly to reach safety before they are cut off by the beaters and have to run the gauntlet of the shooting party? I like to think it is, and if it is, are not pheasants more intelligent than I had ever given them credit for? The last one is through the hedge and scurrying across to catch up with its colleagues and I continue my journey. The turnips haven't grown since last week and I return the way I came. There's not a pheasant to be seen. Should I tell the keeper what I've seen? I decide the pheasants' little secret is safe with me, you have to admire ingenuity.

★★★

The sequence of main conversation topics in the pub has nearly run its 12-month course. We are all well into our winter feeding routines now and there is less day-to-day anecdotal excitement, the main recurring theme for a few weeks now has been about shooting, but already one or two have mentioned getting their ewes scanned after Christmas. Most of them around the table do a little bit of shooting but they all like to go beating and they all have their 'beating' stories to tell.

There always used to be a clear social divide on shooting days between the guns and the rest of the people involved who made it all happen. This still exists in many places and I've always suspected that some people who shoot actually enjoy the deference that is shown to them as much as the shooting.

There was a piece on television the other night about Scott of the Antarctic. Although they were trapped in some sort of icehouse for months on end in appalling conditions, there was still an imaginary line on the floor that separated officers and men. That still exists today in some places.

I've always felt comfortable either side of the line but if I had to choose, I'd go with the men. It's a bit like a lounge bar and a saloon bar, as a friend once said, 'You'll never find someone to help you cart bales in a lounge bar.' But the shoot where those around the table go treats everyone the same, it's just that some have guns and some have sticks, but they all eat and drink together and the social parts of the day out, they all enjoy.

As an aside, I've decided not to go shooting anymore. I used to do a lot but life moves on and I enjoy other things more now. If it's a terrible cold day with a howling wind, sitting in a warm kitchen writing is one of those things.

★★★

It's my grumpy time of year. I don't like Christmas and so I do my best grumpy behaviour. But I have to melt a bit for my grandchildren and not spoil their excitement and some of what goes on I sneakingly enjoy, but I don't admit it. Despite my best attempts I can get caught up in some of it, the general feeling of goodwill, the decorations, the trees. But the flashing lights around here are blue and fixed to the top of police cars.

December 31st 2011

I have to buy 'stuff' this winter to feed the cattle. It's to replace the stuff (silage) that didn't grow because of the drought we suffered in this area. I could buy stock-feed potatoes, and there are plenty about, they are a sort of second-quality potato. If there are plenty of potatoes about, as there are this year, the second-quality can be really good; we've been eating them in the house for weeks. Silage and hay are much too expensive because they are short for the same obvious reason but what I have been buying this week is fodder beet. These are big swede-like mangold-like roots and once the cattle get used to them, which takes a couple of days, they eat them with such relish that it does you good just to watch them enjoying their food.

Watching the cattle really content is one of the pleasures of farming. I found the beet about four miles away but as ever it isn't quite that simple. You have to go and weigh your empty tractor and trailer at the weighbridge, put your beet on, go back and weigh it again and then, the biggest job, persuading the vendor that all subsequent loads will be about the same so you don't have to go the extra miles to the weighbridge every time. One of the reasons it takes cattle a couple of days to get into them is that they have to work out how to eat them. When we put the first lot out in the feed troughs there was a lot of sniffing and inspecting going on. But one heifer worked it out right away.

She latched onto a beet as big as a rugby ball and started to eat it. Because cattle only have teeth on the bottom jaw they don't bite lumps off, they sort of shave it with those bottom teeth leaving a flat plane. It was a picture, about 16 cattle either side of the passageway all focused on this one heifer. They knew by the noise that she was eating something as well but they couldn't work out how she was doing it. I've rarely seen anything or anybody get such undivided attention.

★★★

It all starts with a fairly innocent conversation about crops. Stuff like, 'Our winter barley is looking well,' and 'The wheat we put in last looks better than our early wheat.' Then it comes 'You got any swedes this time?' They are all on full alert now. They all say they haven't got any swedes this year but I know they have. (They pronounce it swids round here.)

'You got any swids?' The one who has asked the question is very partial to a swede but he doesn't grow any himself. This is more a technicality as he sees other people's swedes as part of nature's bounty. I know people who will choose where they grow their swedes just in the hope that he won't be able to spot them from the road. But spot them he usually does and dines on them most days. But he's a generous man and if someone is foolish enough to grow swede next to the road, he will happily get you some. 'You like swedes? I'll get you some swedes.' He's even been known to give bags of swedes for Christmas presents, which is kind and thoughtful, and the recipients, overwhelmed by his generosity, feel obliged to give him a present in return. That's why they all shake their heads when he asks if they've got any swedes. But they all know he doesn't believe them.

★★★

Our corgi is not like a royal corgi. Royal corgis are bigger and plumper. Some Royal corgis are obviously crossed with dachshunds. Our corgi isn't crossed with anything and I've got the paperwork to prove it. But I've never trusted paperwork and to be honest, our corgi looks like a cross between a fox and a meerkat. She's low to the ground, so she likes to sit on vantage points and bark at things like the cats and the sun, but she's always busy about the yard and you never know where you'll find her. And she's got a long bushy tail.

So I'm feeding the calves one morning and I spot the corgi curled up fast asleep in one of the empty pens. She doesn't move when I arrive, which is unusual, so after I've fed the calves I wake her up. But it isn't a corgi, it's a fox, a little light-coloured vixen, looks a bit like a cross between a fox and a meerkat: she gets up, stretches, yawns, and leaves the shed in her own time and goes outside, climbs up on a pile of muck and goes back to sleep in the sun. And people say they don't release 'tame' town foxes in the countryside! She was there for three days on the trot and then disappeared again.

★★★

I'm talking to a shopkeeper from our small local town. I ask her what Christmas has been like for business. She says it's been a disaster. I can't get a feel for how business has actually been. I think it may have been OK but she's not letting on. I saw a disaster the other day: I think you call them a tableau. It wasn't a nativity play, it was a nativity scene with real people and lots of Christmassy music all designed to put shoppers in a good mood and to spend more money. The organizer paid £190 for a donkey. I say that £190 was very reasonable for a donkey, that I used to keep donkeys and wouldn't mind having a couple more but I thought £500 apiece was too dear but £190 was good. 'She didn't buy the donkey; she paid £190 to hire it for one day!' (That makes £500 look cheap to buy one). The community all had to chip in to pay for it. 'Not only that, Mary turned out to be a chain smoker and we couldn't get Joseph out of the pub.' It's starting to make my Christmas seem simple. 'And she left hay and straw all over the place outside the town hall and guess who had to clear it up?' I've heard enough, I'm off.

January 7ᵀᴴ 2012

Last year I took one look at the list of Christmas cards I was supposed to send, dumped them in the bin and sent a cheque to a charity called *Operation Smile*, that operates on children with cleft palates. I've done the same again this year but in addition we decided to have a charity event at the pub between Christmas and New Year. On 27th December we had a pram race, from one end of the village to the other. I'm still overwhelmed by the support we had. Ours is a tiny village but there must have been 250–300 people out on the main road. The support from local people and businesses was amazing. We did it for the charity I have mentioned and raised over £3,000, enough for 20 operations. Our intention was to make children smile for the rest of their lives not just for Christmas.

***

I have to explain some of the stuff I write. If you are from a farming background you will understand immediately but if not, I need to set the scene. I knew a good storyteller once who always started with: 'Picture the scene'. Well, we've got this shed where we house 48 cows. They lie on a straw bed and then there's a clear strip of concrete where they stand to feed at a barrier. Their silage and soya mix is put out for them along the barrier and the roof of the shed extends out a few feet to keep the food dry. So the feed is put out every morning and all the cows are feeding in a long row. A small procession goes down the silage and it's Neville the cockerel and Lucy, his common-law wife. Lucy leads the way, pecking away at bits of corn she can find. Neville is close behind. As they progress slowly along, most of the cows pull back to allow them to pass; if they don't pull back, Neville gives them a sharp peck on the nose. There's a third member of the procession, our corgi. She walks slowly alongside Neville, and every couple of feet Neville aims a peck at her, but he never makes contact, the corgi just moves her head a few inches and is totally undeterred by the danger of his beak. She follows cockerel and hen closely all morning as they go about their business. Sometime in the late morning, Lucy will find a cosy spot to lay an egg. The corgi is on it in a flash and carries it away to eat. She leaves cock and hen alone then, until next morning that is.

***

We had our staff Christmas meal, which sounds a bit grand but anyone who helps us gets invited and it includes a full spectrum of society. One of our helpers used to be the district's most serious drinker. When he was in his early 30s the doctor bet him £20 that if he didn't stop drinking he wouldn't live until he was 40. So on his 40th birthday he made an appointment to see the same doctor, claimed the £20 and had drunk most of it by lunchtime. It was this story that we were laughing about at the Christmas meal. He's quite sensible with his drinking now, but he was telling us that when he was at his most serious stage in his drinking, and had the money, he would drink ten pints and then ten shots off what he calls the top shelf most nights. Which makes most of us look very sensible indeed. Later on the conversation turned to age. He was asked how old he was: '55,' he says. Someone said, 'You don't look it, I didn't think you were that old.' 'Ah well,' he says, 'I've always looked after myself.'

***

Some people I know think that I live out in the sticks. This isn't completely true; we live further out than that, which is roughly out in the sticks and then a bit further on. There are a lot of advantages to this, a way of life in a friendly tranquil environment. But there's one disadvantage: drinking and driving. Because of where we live and because there's hardly any traffic and lots of people's journey home from the pub is on unclassified roads, there's a temptation to have just one more. The disadvantage is that police cars crawl all over the area and if you do meet a car it's likely to have a blue light on the top.

A local policeman once told me that it was common practice for his colleagues that came on duty at ten o'clock at night to head for the hills as quickly as they could. The theory was that if they could catch some old farmer driving home and breathalyse him, by the time he had been taken to the nick and processed, it would be so late, everyone else was home and in bed. If, however, the police stayed in a town centre, they would have youths throwing cans at the car and then they would have to chase them and given the waistline of most of the policemen around here, couldn't catch them anyway, no, so much better to chase an old farmer on his way home in a Land Rover. I'm not defending drinking and driving here, I don't do it myself. I go to the pub a lot and I've drunk so much cranberry juice there can't be many cranberries left.

Anyway, a local man calls in to an isolated pub on his way home, 'I'll just have one on the way home' – they all say that. But by eight o'clock he's got a real wobble on. He asks the other regulars if they think he'll be OK to drive. Sensing an opportunity for some fun, they tell him he'll be OK if he takes a few sensible precautions.

Firstly he has to dilute the alcohol so they persuade him to drink ten pints of cold water. He does this with a bit of a struggle but he's still the worse for the drink he's consumed so they tell him that now he's got to take the alcohol out of his breath and that he best way to do that is to eat some English mustard. The landlord fetches three jars of mustard from the kitchen and slowly he eats the three pots. Nearly ready to drive now they tell him but he's still a bit unsteady on his feet. Nothing better for steadiness than chrysanthemums they tell him so he eats three bunches of chrysanthemums and for good measure they get him to drink the water out of the vases. Then someone drives him home, which is what they intended to do all along. So this story has a happy ending. I like happy endings.

JANUARY 14TH 2012

The festive season is gone now and normal working is resumed on the farm. It was about 25° warmer over the period than it was 12 months ago, which is just fine. But I'm left with a strange feeling. I seemed to be so busy, I forgot to be grumpy. So there's all this grumpiness still inside me and I'm not sure whether it will just dissolve or will it still have to come out somehow? I might try to let it just simmer away inside me; I'm sure I will be able to use it sometime in the future.

There weren't many of us in the pub one night. It was the evening of New Year's Day and it wouldn't be difficult to work out why the pub was quiet. The lights were still on when we started milking that morning and they were still on when we finished! Anyway, for some reason the conversation turned to recycling and, as we were in the pub, to recycling bottles in particular. I've always been a recycling sceptic, if recycling means eliminating waste I'm all for it but if recycling means sending lorries around rural areas picking up grass cuttings and leaves, just how wasteful is that, when both products could be easily accommodated under the nearest hedge?

The couple of younger people in the conversation are enthusiastic recyclers and sense I am a sceptic. You don't have to be that perceptive to sense that. So I tell them that 'when I was a boy' all bottles were recycled. The 'when I was a boy' bit gets eyes rolling upwards, but as it's my round they want to know more about it, particularly as they are young and they see recycling as young and they, part of it. 'Every bottle went back to be reused'

I tell them. They don't believe me and want to know how it worked. 'Simple, there was a deposit on the bottle so they all went back to where they came from, milk bottles were reckoned to go out refilled eight times and I suspect that would be the life of most bottles.' They are quite impressed. If you want to drive change, there's nothing like money to drive it.

The best bit of recycling I ever did was nicking beer barrels at the back of the pub and taking them to another pub and getting the deposits on them. Already there are cracks appearing in the Holy Grail of recycling, they've stopped taking cardboard around here and there's some plastic they won't take soon. I'm not really interested, most things came out of the ground and perhaps that's where they were intended to end up. What does interest me is what people put out to be recycled. At a glance you can now look in a green container and see what they drink. It can be quite surprising: it's not all young girls in skimpy tops that are doing all the drinking. There's more than a bottle of wine going every day in lots of households. Doesn't affect me, I don't drink in the house. If you came around here and it was an appropriate time of day I would offer you a drink and I have drink to offer you. But I go to the pub because I enjoy the company and the gossip and I share it with you, so you can all stay at home drinking cheap supermarket beer and wine, but don't come to me complaining when your local pub shuts down.

★★★

Most of the land we farm, we rent, and consequently the shooting goes with the landlord. The eighty acres where we live we own - well the bank owns it really - they just let us live here, and for what little it's worth, we have the shooting. It's not enough to be a shoot, we've got a wood of about an acre where there are always a few pheasants and we have an area around the poultry sheds where we had to create a bank, to shield the sheds from view. We planted 2,000 trees on the bank. If you live in an area where there is a bit of commercial shooting, and you don't shoot yourselves, you can inadvertently create a sanctuary.

The area around the poultry sheds has become just that; there are always pheasants there, sometimes 40 or 50. We don't really want them there, we have footbaths outside both sheds but there is always an outside chance of stepping in pheasant poo and carrying an infection into the sheds and creating a problem. So we let the next-door shoot go over our land. They drive the pheasants out of the cover afforded by the trees around the poultry sheds and keep the numbers down which is fine by us, and they get another drive out of our wood, which is the stopping-off point as pheasants drift down from the estates where they were reared.

So every ten days or so all these vehicles turn up on our yard carrying the guns (the shooters), the beaters, and more dogs than you've ever seen. It's a bit like some army on the move. Spaniels and Labradors decamp from the back of trucks and some look to fight, some to make love, either activity encouraging shouts of disapproval from respective owners. Is there any other animal that shows as much energy as a spaniel? It's only a farmyard but they are away, heads down, noses glued to the ground as they circle around looking for scent.

This is corgi territory but she is wary of all the noise and activity and does all her barking at a distance. One spaniel, a bit busier than the others disappears in to the calf shed. But he's not there long before there's a yelp. This may be corgi territory, but it's also cockerel country. A yelp can be very eloquent. Its main purpose is to convey the receipt of pain, but it can also convey surprise, as is the case this time. The afflicted spaniel scurries out of the calf shed, its tail between its legs.

He's followed by Neville our cockerel who stands at the entrance of the shed, flaps his wings and crows defiantly. His is a very clear message: 'Anyone else fancy his chances?' The spaniel stops at a safe distance and looks back in bewilderment. He's been chasing birds all morning, that's his job, but this one has fought back. There's a speck of blood on the end of his nose. The other dogs seem to get the message and don't go near. The shooting party move towards the poultry sheds, there are loud calls to go quietly, which is ironic, because five minutes ago it sounded as if a circus had just come to town.

JANUARY 28TH 2012

Today I take you gently up to your knees in slurry. Most cows lie down in what we call cubicles; in North America they call them 'free stalls' which is probably a better description of the same thing, simply because it sounds better. It's a place where they can go and rest whenever they like on a comfortable bed. Ours lie on a comfortable bed of deep sand.

Cows like to lie down quite a lot and should they feel the need to lift their tails and evacuate the remains of the large quantities of food they eat, the cubicles are designed so that this excreta (we don't call it that) falls outside the comfortable bed onto the concrete passage. This is a very important design feature because otherwise the cow would be lying in 'it' and getting herself very dirty and as her udder is at that end as well, the udder would get dirty and we don't want dirty udders for clean milk production, do we? So 'it' falls on the concrete passageway and twice a day we gather it all up along with all the other excreta that the herd has produced whilst walking about to feed and be milked and we call this slurry, which is an easier word than excreta. We gather it up with a sort of squeegee thing on the back of a tractor which we call a scraper. It is logical that the tractor that pulls the scraper is called a scraper tractor.

Some people call scraping a chore but I have personally taken scraping to such a high level that it has become an art form and I take great pride in the skill I bring to it. The scraper tractor is usually the oldest tractor on the farm, ours is 40, and it is invariably covered with that same stuff that you try to keep off the cows. If slurry was a lubricant, scraper tractors would last forever. A really authentic scraper tractor will have an old Land Rover wheel on one of its front corners.

So we gather all this slurry together and push it into what we call a lagoon. Our lagoon is a great big hole in the ground that will hold several weeks' supply of slurry. I'm not sure why we call it a lagoon because there are no palm trees around the outside and the only blue water that gets in there is the discarded water from the cows' copper foot baths. So we have all this slurry and from time to time we suck it out with tankers and spread it on the land and it's good for the land because it grows the next crop.

So we come to this week. Dry crisp frosty weather, fields firm and dry, lovely, perfect even, for spreading slurry. And that's what we've been doing. The fields are so dry the tractor and tanker don't leave a mark on the grassland. It's so dry we don't bring any mud back out on the road. With fertiliser well over £300 a ton we are saving on the amount we have to buy. If we buy less, we reduce our carbon footprint: there are so many plusses to the story, it ticks so many boxes that it's a really good scenario. But not for much longer. The world of slurry is just about to go crazy.

Enter the world of NVZ. Nitrate Vulnerable Zones. This is an EEC directive designed to reduce nitrogen in ground water and water courses. Briefly it stops you going out on perfect days like this week I have just described and spreading slurry; it makes you store it and you can only start spreading after a certain date. Not all the country is designated NVZ. We are not sure in this valley, because 'they' tried to get us in a few years ago and we won our appeal – we all had to put £1,000 in a kitty – and now they are trying to get us in again. It's such a crazy law. Nitrate levels are falling in water, so it's not needed. Where it was needed was in places like Holland with its intensive dairy and pig units and high water tables, but we get dragged along with them with the EEC ethos of 'one size fits all'.

I know lots of dairy farmers who will not put up new facilities to store slurry that cost, say, £100,000, because they are no better off. It will just be more weight on the millstone of borrowing they already have around their neck. Those that do will be waiting for the due date for spreading to arrive and then the world and his muck-spreader will be out turning the world as we know it brown, as they race to get slurry on to spring crops.

A few years ago there was an east wind and throughout East Anglia they could smell the Dutch spreading their slurry. Even if our farmers throughout East Anglia spread it in good conditions, if there were a downpour the next week, there would be so much slurry on the ground that some would get washed into water courses making the water vulnerable. These massive risks are not there with the sensible scenario we have now. What really disappoints me is that a couple of years ago when I was even more important than I think I am now, I went to a Conservative party briefing of agriculturists, before the general election, in Westminster. They gave us a clear impression that they thought the NVZ rule was ridiculous; they had a derogatory name for it. But now that they have a power of sorts, all that is forgotten.

I was talking to a man who manages a large urban farm for a local authority where they have hundreds of thousands of visitors a year. He keeps a herd of 60 Jerseys but has been told to reduce them to 25 so that the farm complies with the NVZ ruling. They have enough slurry storage for 25 cows but not for 60. They didn't need storage for 60 because they would go out and spread some in nice dry winter weather like we all do. 'Trouble is' he tells me, '25 won't be a viable unit and I can see them all being sold before long, which is a pity because these town children just love to see the cows being milked.'

And that, in a nutshell, is the NVZ dilemma facing most dairy farmers: borrow lots of money, reduce cow numbers significantly, or stop milking altogether. I suspect that a lot will choose the latter two options.

Meanwhile my slurry tanker is taking two loads an hour of valuable nutrients out onto the fields, and not doing anything but good. So what happened to common sense?

FEBRUARY 4TH 2012

Have you ever inadvertently trodden on a piece of wood that has a nail sticking out of it? I did it once, the pain is terrible. I had to get someone to pull the piece of wood out of my foot, and that's not the end of it; the pain doesn't go away for several days. In bed at night it throbs away, much like an injury in a cartoon film: you can't see it, but it feels as if it is visibly moving. For a long time afterwards you make sure there are no more bits of wood about with nails sticking out.

A friend of mine had the same accident last week, trod on a nail, so he turned up at the doctors. I suppose he should have gone to A&E but that's 45 minutes away and the doctors is only five minutes. They refused to see him, well, they would, wouldn't they, he hadn't got an appointment. It was only when he took his welly off and tipped some blood onto the reception carpet that they took pity on him and pushed him in to see the doctor. Not that there's a lot you can do except clean it up a bit and take a handful of painkillers, and be more careful where you put your feet in future.

★★★

We've rented some more buildings. They are three miles away in a different direction to those journeys we routinely travel. We have to go through the village which is usually interesting both for me and for Mert the dog. I stare at the people we see and he

barks at the dogs they have with them. I'm at the stage in my life
when I need to have some glasses with me at all times in case I
need to read something, these are usually hanging on a piece of
string around my neck. So yesterday the dog and I set off with a
big bale of straw on a machine that throws the straw, shredded,
into a shed for the cattle to lie on. I can tell that the dog enjoys
these journeys because he's on the cab floor by my feet, but he's
sitting up looking out of the window.

As we get to the village I slow down, the better to see who
is about and I put my glasses on for the same reason. But it's still
before nine o'clock and there's no one about yet and the dog gives
a sort of sigh and decides to lie down. He's a bit of a lump since
he had his operation of a very private nature and he flops himself
down on the accelerator, and we are away. The machine on the
back is heavy when it's got a bale in it and the tractor front wheels
actually come off the ground for a few yards. The quick way to
get him off the accelerator is to kick him, but this is also a quick
way to get bitten, so as I race through the village I stroke his back
and eventually he sits up again so I can stroke his head, and peace
and dignified progress is restored. In the pub that night someone
says 'You were in a bit of a rush this morning,' I tell them, 'With
a workload like mine, there's no time to hang about.'

FEBRUARY 18TH 2012

A local wildlife group is organising evening walks to the wood
for people to witness ravens roosting. Some members of the group
tell me that there are 200 ravens there and decide the sight is
spectacular. Local farmers reckon there are 400 ravens there, so
for the purpose of this particular story, and without any accurate
figures, we will agree that there are a lot. The wildlife group and
the farmers may or may not agree on the numbers issue and it's for
sure that their views on the advantages of these large numbers will
be at opposites. I have to come down on the side of the farmers. I

mix with farmers, I am obviously a farmer as well, I sit with the farmers in the pub, whereas the members of the wildlife group probably drink cheap supermarket wine at home, but to be fair, if the pub is threatened with closure, they will fight to save it.

Me, I'd actually like to go and see the ravens roosting but a greater concern is the imbalance these numbers cause when such a huge number of predators are concentrated in one area. They continue to prey on sheep. If a ewe should get onto its back, something that occasionally happens because of the weight of its fleece, it will soon lose its eyes and probably its teats. If it is lambing outside, whilst recumbent in the lambing position, it can lose its eyes and the lamb can lose its eyes and tongue before it is even fully born. I know I've told you this before and I'm telling you again because it is still going on. I don't know if the ravens will disperse as they seek nest sites but whatever happens, there could be even more next year. It's a distressing issue for farmers whose sheep suffer from attacks and I am bewildered that wildlife groups cannot come to terms with the fact that it is possible for numbers of a species to become excessive and upset the natural balance. I have heard it suggested that, should a sheep die of natural causes, it should be left in the field to provide a food source for the ravens, but it is illegal to leave a carcass in the field and there are plenty of people about in the countryside who will report you if you do. What no one seems to address is why all these ravens are there and where did they come from?

There is no doubt in my mind at all that they are a by-product of large commercial shoots. This is dangerous ground for me because I rent ground off people with large commercial shoots but if you think about it, if someone rears tens of thousands of pheasants on a commercial scale, all through the summer there will be pheasants that don't make it that are hoovered up by scavengers like chick-rearing ravens. There are the pheasants that we all see run over on the road.

And when winter comes, the most challenging time of year for all wild species, they go out six days a week and shoot pheasants until the end of January, so scavengers can live very well on the injured birds that pick up a pellet or two, but are not located by the dogs. I'm not a fan of large commercial shoots and I'm not a fan of too many ravens, but I do think I have a balanced view.

★★★

They are strange things, feathers. Some people have an aversion to them. And for those people, not just the sort of dislike that says 'I don't like feathers,' it's the sort of aversion that makes their skin crawl, sends them into shudders of revulsion. And because they don't like feathers, they don't like birds, because most birds I come across have lots of feathers. I sometimes say to someone, 'We had new chicks in yesterday, would you like to see them?' 'No thank you, I don't like feathers.'

I was feeding the calves one Saturday afternoon and a calf jumped over the gate. You have to open the gate to get it back in and that is an open invitation to the other calves to get out as well. So I fetch my number two grandson (not in preference but order of age) out of the house to help. 'I'll stop the calves getting out and if you sneak down the side of the stock trailer, you'll be behind the calf that has just got out and we'll get her back in.' There were about four pullets in the stock trailer waiting to be collected and my grandson refused point blank to squeeze past the trailer because of the feathers.

I told him, I cursed him, I tried to push him, but there was no way he would go. So he had to go another way around and we were chasing the calf for a quarter of an hour instead of two or three minutes.

I have an aversion to cotton wool. It's not a big problem in my life and I can't remember the last time our paths crossed, but

I simply can't bear to touch it. My grandchildren, on discovering this, have in turn sneaked up on me and put cotton wool on my hands or face and taken great delight in my reaction. Many years ago my wife made a mince pie filled with cotton wool. She never did it again.

★★★

In the pub we often talk about our cockerel Neville and his latest escapades. He has a notoriety that he would probably be proud of: all the pub regulars know about Neville and often ask how he is. So it's the last day of the shooting season, a season that is supposed to finish at the end of January but for some reason, seems to drag on until the 1st February. The vehicles associated with the local shoot all arrive on our yard with all their dogs accompanied by the whistles and the shouts. They seem to be extra animated today and I assume that the extra noise is because it is the last day of the season, but it's not, they are nearly all gathered around a truck and that's where most of the shouts and laughter are coming from. One of the beaters is steadfastly refusing to get out. 'I'm not getting out in this yard, I've heard all about that cockerel.' He lives six miles away, has lived and worked on farms all his life, but he doesn't get out, he sits there until they return and move on to their next drive. If he knew all this, Neville would be very pleased with himself. I go and have a word with the man in the truck. 'Why don't you come out?' 'You must be joking, look at the feathers on that cockerel's neck!'

FEBRUARY 25TH 2012

I love our corgi dearly but when they handed out corgi good looks, she was well at the back of the queue. To start with, she has a long tail. Long tails don't suit corgis, they don't suit a lot of dogs either, but that's for another debate. She's too small for a proper corgi, (which is why I suspect that there's either a touch of fox or meerkat in her DNA), and if I were to be picky, and I am, I would prefer her to be a darker brown. To conclude her physical appraisal, if they were to do a remake of that film *The King's Speech*, she would never make it as an extra. But what she lacks in looks, she makes up for in character: but just lately she has blossomed and now has a shiny coat, put on some weight, is a different corgi, a sleek corgi, a banker-who-has-just-had-a-big-bonus sort of corgi. So we have to wonder, why this transformation? And we investigate.

To start with, she wants to be off out of the kitchen as soon as I get up, and when I let her out, she's off up the yard at some speed. I usually return a bit later to my pen and A4 pad, but Stephen who works here can complete the story, he has a vested interest in the tale, as we shall see. Our corgi makes straight for the calf pens where Neville the cockerel and Lucy his partner roost on a gate. She sits patiently there until, with much crowing and flapping of wings, Lucy and Neville start their day. And off they go, a little procession: hen, cock, corgi, searching for their breakfast, the corgi patiently following their every move.

The highlight of the day is sometime between ten and eleven o'clock. Lucy settles down to lay an egg. Cockerel and corgi stand guard. Egg laid, the birds carry on their meanderings, and the corgi seizes the egg, just yards in front of Stephen, who regards a daily egg as a perk of his job. The corgi always wins the race, the egg is safely in her mouth and she's away, she's in fox mode now, it's a sort of high-speed slink with Stephen shouting at her. She eats the egg on the kitchen doorstep. There's eggshell everywhere, along with all the other bits of stick, plastic and other debris she has found and carried home. Anything that is supposed to be around the house, she carries the other way, back up the yard. This includes boots, shoes, slippers, gloves, hats, some never to be found again.

***

Dogs are a big part of my life. I've been carting muck most of the week. I've been taking it a fair way so I've only managed about a load an hour. I've not taken Mert my sheepdog because he sits on the floor of the cab and his leg is always under the foot throttle and I can only go at half speed. So he sits there on the yard, out in the rain, snow, frost, whatever, and as I come up the yard each time he gets up and wags his tail and gives me this imploring look that clearly says, 'Can I come on the next load?' By mid afternoon I feel a complete bastard so I relent and he gets on with me, and so I only take two more loads instead of three, but so what? The dog positively beams with happiness, I feel better, and anyway I can take that other load tomorrow.

★★★

Just when you think that we've done with shooting and all the shooting stories, we are away again. A game dealer, it is reported, is paying £1 a piece for grey squirrels. Lots of them. 'What's he want them for?' 'He's got an order for them, he wants them for Easter.' There's just a touch of hesitancy over the Easter bit, but as information goes, it seems to suffice. 'Yes but what does he want them for?' 'Someone wants them to eat.' 'Where?' 'They are going to Italy.' There's hesitation again, this time over the word, Italy, in fact it is pronounced very much like a question. This interests me. Grey squirrels never seem to be complete hibernators and on some sunny days, they will be about and could be shot.

The conversation quickly moves on. 'Would you eat a squirrel?' Two in the company say that they already have, the rest say they never would. They are asked to say why, and they find that difficult. Off-hand none of us can think of a cleaner living animal but I suppose those who say they never would, liken a grey squirrel to a rat with a bushy tail. On we go again, 'What's it taste like?' We can all guess the answer. 'Tastes like chicken.' This reminds me of Terry Wogan discussing road kill on breakfast radio – 'tastes like chicken' covered everything from foxes to crows. But there is a qualification for grey squirrel: 'Tastes like chicken with a nutty flavour.' Well, it would, wouldn't it? I suspect that the last speaker has watched too many cooking programmes on television.

What really interests me, as I ponder the grey squirrel for £1 scenario, is just how far this will go. Most dramatic change is quite simply driven by money. There wouldn't be as many wind turbines about if they weren't subsidised so it's the subsidy money that creates the wind turbine farms. And if there was a good price on a grey squirrel and their numbers were decimated, what chance the red squirrel making a comeback in 50 years' time? I'm a bit of a dreamer, I doubt if it will happen, but wouldn't it be nice?

Spring

Red meat is bad for you. We all know that, they've been telling us for years. So why, I ask myself, is meat, red meat, more expensive than it has ever been before? I'm not really in the beef trade and nowhere near sheep trade, but it all has a knock on effect. Store cattle, which are cattle that still have to grow on before they are ready for the food chain, have never been more expensive, dairy cows that have finished their productive lives have never been worth more money and so it goes on, so that the calves I sell to be reared for beef are dearer than I have ever seen before.

I was in a market the other day and couldn't believe what calves were selling for. We sell a lot of calves at home now and there is a real danger of under-selling them. One of my friends was selling store cattle last week and he had a particular bullock that he hoped would make £950. It made £1,160, way beyond his expectations.

Sheep are enjoying a similar boom, driven in this case largely by the prices paid for old ewes. When an old ewe was worth perhaps £10, she would be kept on to produce one more lamb; now she could be worth £70-£90 so off she goes for slaughter and there are less lambs about.

These high prices are not a bonanza for farmers, they are just catch-up to where food prices should really be. If you index-linked food prices over the last 20 years you will see that we've had a low cost food policy that has hopefully come to an end. In the case of sheep, the prices are driven by the value of old ewes, but it's also said that the mutton from old ewes is the only trade that the supermarkets aren't involved in and they can't influence what is happening.

There's an irony in all this: milk hasn't had this boom in prices. Dairy farmers are benefiting from better cull cow and calf prices but milk prices are driven by supermarkets using price formulae, and they are quite likely to try to drop the price of milk because we are getting more money elsewhere.

★★★

Discuss declining bird populations anywhere, particularly in the media, and it's always down to farmers. We are a sort of minority, so we are an easy shot; it's easy to blame us because there's not so many of us to fight back. If it's all our fault, it's something of a contradiction when you hear the farmers and farm workers discussing the lapwings in the pub. The flock of 20-30 seems to have dispersed around the area in pairs and the location of these pairs is followed with interest. 'We' have a pair, and we look out for them every day, we tell each other if we've seen them, we actually take pride in having them about. We will watch out for where they choose to nest, and if we find their eggs we will put a marker nearby so that nothing we do will damage them or disturb the birds whilst they incubate their eggs. I'm not really bothered about the general level of criticism that we attract: most of it comes from people without real lives; we just get on with what we do. That includes giving nature a helping hand where we can.

★★★

I don't think that many cockerels go on to achieve the notoriety of our Neville. People ask about him in the pub. He causes great amusement when he attacks people, just as long as you are not the one being attacked. He's so bold and aggressive that he can be quite scary. It's OK if there's a stick handy but there rarely is. But it's just been half term here, lots of children about, and then it's not so funny. When he attacks me, most of the damage is between knee and bum, but that's face high on a young child and that could be serious. He can draw blood on your leg through jeans and overalls so you have to assume he could scar a child for life.

He had a go at my youngest granddaughter yesterday and her dad decided that enough was enough and Neville would have to be dispatched to that great hen–house in the sky, but he couldn't catch him. I had mixed feelings about it but could obviously see the sense. I didn't think I'd hear Neville crowing the next day, (my son is well aware of where he roosts), but he's still about. He attacked Stephen, who works for us, this morning. I expect he'll be OK now until Easter.

There is an alternative: the current crop of pullets is due to leave us in a couple of weeks' time. There are two cockerels amongst them. If we were to release them onto the yard, would three cockerels be so busy chasing each other that they wouldn't attack people? Then there is the possibility that they would form a gang and we would be attacked by three cockerels at a time. There's only one way to find out.

MARCH 10TH 2012

The largely dry weather has meant that we are starting to get about the fields more as we start our spring work and the winter workload that has kept us mostly around the buildings is added to that of spring work and makes for a very busy time. In the previous two springs we have had long dry spells and in each case the farmers were saying they have lambs a month old that have yet to feel rain on their backs.

★★★

I once saw a feature on the havoc wrought on inland waterways by cormorants. There are 20 on a lake near where I live. An efficient hunter in the wrong place, the cormorant belongs back at the seaside. Where they are now, they upset all sorts of balances but because they are birds, that's OK. A local wildlife group has discovered 'my' hares. So now they are promoting walks across my top ground along public footpaths to see 'Brown hares and buzzards'. If they'd gone there five years ago it would have been a walk to see, 'Brown hares and skylarks', but it seems they currently prefer buzzards. With a bit of common sense, it could have been 'hares, buzzards and skylarks' but if you've got your head in a paper bag, you can't see that and don't want to see it, anyway.

MARCH 17TH 2012

I've found out where the flock of lapwings spend most of their time. It is in a small field just the other side of the buildings I rent. It's only 100 yards away and I'm fascinated that there's such a large group (25-30) together, but I won't even go to look at them. To me, that's important. They need to be left alone. The farmer who owns the field is also leaving them alone, he's being paid to do just that and I'm sure we would all consider that money well spent. A group of this size is so precious, it's difficult to put a value on it. I just wish that we could go that bit further and put some gamekeepers to look after them. The field where they live has all the prerequisites of successful rearing. I'm told lapwing chicks need water within 24 hours of hatching, and that is available. If the group were properly looked after, they could double or treble in size if they had a successful spring. Fast-forward five years and that starts to make a real difference, money well spent. It's a strange scenario.

People who write regularly in the press about nature and wildlife are usually revered. I write a lot about nature and wildlife but as far as I know I'm the only one who advocates direct action against predators in order to give some species a bit of a help where it is needed. So if we take these lapwings as a specific example, I know of plenty of gamekeepers who would protect them. They would trap magpies, shoot the crows, keep the foxes away by trapping them, shoot the badgers and ravens if they were allowed to and I bet, but I don't bet, so I'll guarantee, we, and

I will include myself in this because it's my idea, we would rear more lapwings than anything else that is being done now. It won't happen because the people who could do something can't see it.

★★★

One of my neighbours passed away recently. I was expecting it to be a big funeral. Not particularly wanting to stand in a churchyard for over an hour, I took my seat in church an hour before the appointed time, and there were 20 there before me. With 40 minutes to go, they were already putting people in the choir stalls. That would be no good to me; I don't like to be up at the front. I always sat at the back at school and it always served me well. Then ten minutes to go and the 'newcomers' start to arrive, you can tell by their faces that they think people standing outside are out there for a cigarette, so they push through the throng and can't believe that there's not a seat for them and they have to go back out. They only live perhaps 100 yards away, they can't come to terms with the fact that one person could have so many friends, they can't come to terms with a big country funeral.

★★★

'People' say to me that I don't realise how lucky I am to live where I do because it's so beautiful. Well I do, and I hope that this comes over in my writings. But as I go about my daily travels I can't believe just how much litter is thrown out of cars to end up on grass verges. I can return on a tractor over roads I travelled just an hour earlier and there on the road are fresh cartons, plastic bottles and paper. Traffic movement blows it back onto the verges where it will remain for weeks, a visible scar on our landscape. In London recently, the litter was almost wall-to-wall on main routes and somehow that was not unexpected given the volume of traffic and the people. But around here it seems terrible; to me anyway. What a dirty, untidy nation we have become.

★★★

It amuses me when the dog squares up to visitors; it amuses me when he gives them a bit of a nip. It's not so funny when he nips me, which is once a week when I put the wheely bin out. He gets quite excited when I'm dragging a wheely bin up the yard, probably because I do it at night when I come home from the pub and I wake him up. Which brings my thoughts to Neville the cockerel. I'm a bit worried about his future. Will he survive Easter when there are more children about and he could do real harm? He's such a character, such a part of our farming family that I would miss him.

I went to get what we call our scraper tractor out the other day. Neville was standing guard by it. I didn't have anything to throw at him, I tried to shove him out of the way but he wasn't for moving. In the end I had to rush past him, just me and Neville in a two-foot space, scary stuff. He doesn't move, he just eye-balls me. With some relief I get on the tractor and prepare to start it, but I'm not safe yet, he's up into the tractor with me, striking at me with his beak. He only gets off when the engine starts, leaving me quite shaken. It's almost as if he set a trap for me. I must get some doors for that tractor cab so he can't follow me.

What of his future? Well, the next batch of pullets is due to go soon, and there are two more cockerels in there. So we catch one and loose him on to the yard. We call him Geoffrey. There's a theory behind this. Will Geoffrey distract Neville from attacking humans? Will he be so preoccupied with a rival for Lucy's affections that his target in future will be Geoffrey and not me or anyone else who crosses his path?

The aim of the theory is that if it works, Neville will live a long life and not be despatched because of the threat he poses to children. The aim is a happy ending. I like happy endings. And it works. Neville doesn't know which way to turn: he can hear

Geoffrey crowing and it drives him to distraction and now he's busy, he's either crowing back, exercising his conjugal rights or flapping his wings in an aggressive display. Success! But not too fast. Geoffrey hasn't been seen for two days.

MARCH 24TH 2012

Watching wildlife from the tractor gives you a unique adventure because wildlife become so used to seeing you going slowly up and down the field all day, it gets on with its business, and I can watch. My first real job out on the tractor all day every spring, is to roll the winter wheat and firm the soil down after it may have lifted with the frost. It's my first job and every year I really look forward to it. Today I'm particularly looking for hares, because to be honest, I haven't seen many about during the winter and I'm getting just a bit concerned. After I've rolled 23 acres I've seen six. Well I think I have, but I'm cynical enough to know that I could have seen one hare six times.

This isn't the reassurance I was looking for and the only answer is to phone the keeper. 'Hares! Boy, have you got some hares! They're still lying up in the woods in the daytime until the crops have grown, but I was out with the lamp last week looking for foxes and I bet I saw 100. One was in season and there was a queue to mate with her.' So that's OK then. But is it? I know farmers who are so tight they can't sleep at night if they think there's a rabbit eating their corn. So I do a piece of mental arithmetic that I've done before. I happen to know that hares weigh around 3½ kilos and sheep weigh 50 kilos. So it's about 15 hares to a sheep and 100 hares is about six sheep. If I allow for the keeper counting hares by lamplight, it could easily be 90 hares, (but then again it could be 120!).

So would I lose sleep if I had six of my neighbour's sheep in my field? It would depend which neighbour it was! I've had one sheep all winter and I haven't stressed about it and I'd rather have 100 hares than none. To be honest my biggest concern is that people are starting to talk about them. There's an organised walk going up there to look at them. Word will get about and the next thing you know, we'll have sporting types with lurchers and greyhounds walking the footpaths, and elsewhere.

★★★

Today I've had another day on the roller. We've just drilled some spring wheat on our very top field and I've been rolling that in. It's a different world up there today: it's very cold, so it's misty and I can hardly see where to drive and the mist has a dampness to it that seems to make it colder still. It was warm enough when I left the yard on our oldest tractor, which is a favourite of mine, but it has no radio and no heater and the cab has a few gaps that let the cold in. There's not a hare to be seen and if they've any sense, they'll be in the shelter of the adjoining woods keeping their heads down. Although I can't see anything, there's a strong wind blowing so I wonder if I'm in mist or up in the clouds.

There's a lot of birds about on the freshly tilled ground, though what they live on, goodness only knows. I can recognise the skylarks as they flutter away on the ground, leading me away from potential nest sites. I'm confident they haven't started to lay yet which is why I want to get this rolling done. There's some other birds I'm not sure of, I think they are field fares but I'll look in my bird book when I get home. I'm not sorry when I finish and I can get down to warmer climes and leave the birds in peace. It's a tough life for them up there with the weather and predators to contend with. They deserve some sort of avian Duke of Edinburgh award.

★★★

Life must be confusing for a dog. My dog, Mert, lives an orderly life. There's people he likes and there's people he doesn't like and he ignores the ones he likes, but not to worry, because the cockerel Neville attacks everybody anyway. Mert particularly likes biting the A.I. man. The A.I. man usually calls at 9-ish and Mert is ready for him, he bites him on his way in and he bites him on the way out, to use a Falklands-type analogy. And for good measure, as he goes, he bites the tyres of the van as well. Where he is confused is that there are times when we are not inseminating cows as we work towards calving cows in batches and there is no A.I. man to terrorise. So what happens to confuse him?

It's only the postman. He turns up early one day, he's got a different van that's on hire, it's white, not silver like the A.I. man's but it's exactly the same make. For some reason the postman has a high vis yellow coat on that I've not seen before. So what's a dog to do with all these mixed messages? Bite him in the bum, that's what he does. Comes as a complete surprise to the postman who usually comes in the 'People Mert Likes category'. He's back in his van before you can say 'recorded delivery'. The bites are really nips, amusing for the spectators but not if it's you that gets nipped.

For real amusement you need to be about when the cattle foot trimmer is here. We put the cows to be treated in a shed and he pulls his truck and cattle crush in there as well. I like to take a cup of tea in to the workshop just opposite and watch what goes on. He's got a very sophisticated crush. A cow walks in and he pushes some buttons and the crush tightens onto the cow and grips it in a warm comfortable embrace. Then he pushes another button and the cattle tips over so that the cow is lying on her side and her four feet are presented for him to work on at a sort of table height.

It's all very sophisticated and professional but he has his problems. Mert doesn't like him. Mert has got his head over the manger and every time the foot trimmer goes to get another cow, Mert lifts his lips and snarls at him, so he has to keep one eye on Mert all the time. Mert is the least of his worries, because Neville doesn't like him either. The foot trimming takes place in Neville territory and about every other cow, he launches an attack from behind, spur and beak hitting his back and legs. I'd like to take my grandchildren to watch, but oh dear, the language.

MARCH 31ST 2012

I have a south-facing grass field that seemed to suffer particularly badly in last year's dry summer. The grass was due to last another 12 months but it's at a stage where it won't really do that and we either have to plough it and start again or try to introduce some grass seed that will bolster it a bit longer. I have a friend who has a drill that will put seed into slits in existing grassland and I asked him to come and have a look one evening to advise me what to do. He came one lovely sunny evening and as we drove slowly to the field he was a typical farmer. We drove past some dry cows and heifers and I could sense that he was counting them. 'Dry cows look well, there's two there that won't be long.' (Meaning that they'll calve soon).

We drive past my bays of straw and it's just the same, he's counting the bales in one bay and multiplying the bays. 'Got a lot of straw left, you could sell some of that, it's worth just over £20 a bale.' It's what farmers do, they are fascinated with what other farmers do, or own or even more importantly, what they haven't done and haven't got. We eventually arrive in the grass field in question. He falls silent immediately and I stop the truck and we just sit there. There are six hares about 30 yards away, up on their haunches watching us watching them. He breaks the silence. 'Don't they look lovely. I haven't seen a hare on our place for ten years.'

★★★

I suppose what I write here is a sort of record of what I see and do in my daily life. I'm not sure about writing this next bit – there are those of you who could, and probably will, take it the wrong way but it's what happens here, so here goes. It's a busy morning and I need a full day on the tractor rolling but it's also the time of year where there are lots of routine jobs to do. Before I can get away I have to put fresh straw into one of the yards. We have a machine that does this and I put a big square bale of wheat straw into it. These bales are about eight feet long and three of them would probably weigh a ton. There are six strings around each bale and the string has to be quite thick. So I'm just removing the last string and not paying particular attention, probably thinking about what I hope to do during the day, when I'm hit by a heavy blow in the back of the knee. It's in the sort of place where kids will knock you so that your knee inadvertently buckles and you nearly fall down.

Except that it isn't a kid, it's Neville and he means serious business. He has me, there's nowhere to run except round and round the tractor. I coil the strings together carefully so that I have a bunch of string in my hand about four feet long, it won't be as effective as a rope because the loose ends are just, well, loose, but it's all I have. He comes in again, spurs raking at my legs, beak striking where it can, and I lash out at him with my string. It's not a very effective weapon but I do manage some telling blows. Man and cockerel fight toe to toe for about ten minutes. Neville is well up for the fight, he's undeterred, he's not taken a backward step. After ten minutes and with no sign of me winning I start to wonder how long this will go on for, because if you remember I'm supposed to be busy. So I back carefully off until I can get on the tractor. Neville's still there, neck feathers fluffed up, ready for more. If I'm honest, and I sometimes am, no one won. But Neville came very close to winning and as he struts nonchalantly away, you can see that he thinks he did. Perhaps I should knot the strings together at the business end next time. That'll teach him.

APRIL 7TH 2012

We're a month earlier this year putting out a magpie trap. We cleaned up the magpies last summer but I suspect that we did it too late to prevent then creating carnage amongst eggs and fledglings. By the end of February there were three pairs of magpies on the farm: from where? I suppose they fill any magpie-free vacuums there are. It's a divisive subject: to leave them or to control them. I see what they can do at first-hand.

Personally, as you know I'm all about balance and giving nature a hand to achieve that balance. In the end it all comes down to choices: do you want buzzards, carrion crows and magpies, of which there are an abundance, or do you want more song birds and more ground-nesting birds which seem to be having a hard time? If you wanted to make my day, it would be for me to hear the call of the curlew one early morning, through the mist, as I fetch the cows in. I know there are lots of factors that affect bird populations but one of them is predation and when I can, I will do something about that. And if, in the fullness of time, magpies become scarce, I'd probably help them as well, leave them some carrion or some eggs. If Neville doesn't alter his ways, which are getting more and more aggressive, he could find himself as a magpie takeaway. But not just yet.

***

A serious contender for the harbinger of spring award is the resurrection of my old Discovery from its winter slumbers. We had put it by in a building for the previous winter where it had become a residence for a rat family. Some men with terriers actually killed 15 rats inside it and we had to wash the rat poo out with a hosepipe. The great wonder was that the rats hadn't eaten any of the wiring. We were not going to take a chance on that again so the Discovery was backed into a suitable patch of nettles when the cows came in in the autumn, and there it remained until last week. Its time had come: it had gone lame on one of its front tyres so we pumped that up, put on the jump leads, and away she went. The windows still won't go up but it's all working otherwise and now it's filled with all the paraphernalia an electric fencer would ever need. We use it to fetch the cows and to move the electric fences every afternoon. Mert the dog is particularly pleased because it's his favourite form of transport and I like it because it's been how we have spent a lot of our lives. It's the A team back together. It just amazes me how you can leave a lump of dilapidated machinery out in all weathers for six months, and it's all up and running again in ten minutes.

April 14th 2012

The only enduring theme in the news this week has been the dry weather. I have had plenty of time to reflect on this as I travel up and down the farm carting chicken muck. I find that, thus far, this spring is a mirror-image of last. Once again I have a field of winter wheat that badly needs a drink, that at the moment doesn't look as if it will get one. We travel, the chicken muck and I, up a track that runs along our boundary. To my left is a field of wheat belonging to my neighbour and to the right is mine. My neighbour's has looked a really good crop ever since it came up, but mine has looked indifferent. Most factors are the same: the main difference was that his went in earlier than mine and that was because mine followed a grass crop and the ground was much too hard to plough any earlier. But a change has taken place with his crop over the last week: it has become yellow, is not growing anymore, it has in effect done what we call, 'gone back'. I get no comfort from this, there's none to be had, mine still looks an indifferent crop crying out for rain, his crop is stressed by the dry weather. And if his crop is struggling, every other crop in every other field is having a hard time. The spring is just so important in terms of the pattern it sets in terms of growth for the rest of the year that the implications are getting more serious by the day. But one of life's lessons is that it's no good agonising over things that you can do nothing about, so I don't, and there's very soon a distraction.

I get to the field where I tip the muck and there's hare activity. There are three hares here and I don't have to be a genius to work out that one is female and two are male and that the males have something else on their minds other than meals, fuel shortages and dry weather. We don't need much imagination to guess what the other two were up to.

April 15th 2012

What a difference a day makes. I got up to a white world and it was snowing hard. It's been an awful cold wet day, rain and sleet from dawn to dusk and some snow settling. But the wheat crops have already changed colour. It's soil temperature that counts, all they needed was a drink.

We let another cockerel, Geoffrey, out on the yard. His purpose was to distract Neville from his attacks on humans. For a couple of days it worked and they worked in a sort of mirror image of each other at a distance of about ten yards, copying each other like a sort of synchronised cockerel walking. Then Geoffrey disappeared. Without trace. Firstly you would suspect a fox but even the most fastidious fox will leave some feathers. So where he is gone no one knows. There was always a chance that the plan wouldn't work; there was always a chance they would gang up together and the attacks would be doubly worse. There is an element of me that hoped this would happen. I didn't want children to be attacked, but the reaction of adults can be very amusing. I already had a name for them. Neville and Geoffrey Kray. But I have to move on. I'm looking in the small ads to buy a turkey stag: now they can be really scary.